**WORSHIP
IN THE
REFORMED
TRADITION**

FREDERICK W. SCHROEDER

WORSHIP IN THE REFORMED TRADITION

UNITED CHURCH PRESS · Philadelphia · Boston

264
Sch7b

162595

Library of Congress Catalog Card Number 66-16194

To Former Students
with whom most of the convictions set forth
in this volume were shared in the classroom.

PREFACE

When I began to teach the basic course in public worship at Eden Theological Seminary, it became necessary to explore and examine the nature, the traditions, and the patterns of worship. Up to that time I had looked upon worship as something to be done rather than as something to be analyzed. The rise of the liturgical movement gave added impetus to a closer examination of the nature of worship. Here and there practices were introduced in the Protestant cultus which hitherto had been unknown. Laymen as well as fellow clergymen began to ask searching questions about liturgical practices and postures that they had either observed or were expected to follow.

This prompted me to examine not only the new departures from traditional patterns of Protestant worship but to examine the Protestant tradition itself. In the course of this study I became more convinced than ever that the cultus of the church must be shaped by theology rather than by tradition. Such a rationale underlies the chapters of this volume.

I am aware that my views are highly critical of some aspects of the liturgical movement, primarily on theological grounds. I am persuaded that the Protestant cultus, with all its varieties and in spite of occasional vagaries, stands squarely within the framework of the Hebrew-Christian conception of God. On that score Protestant Christianity has no need to apologize for its liturgical heritage, nor is there any reason why it should borrow from the classical liturgies of the distant past. Before adapting or adopting practices from pre-Reformation times, Protestants should be sure that what is taken over does not contradict basic biblical principles.

In the course of my reading about worship, I have become indebted to far more writers than I can acknowledge. However, I do want to mention Henry Sloane Coffin who in my judgment incorporated authentic insights and valuable guidelines for Protestant worship in his book *The Public Worship of God*. Among the other books that have been extremely helpful I would list the following: *Worship* by Evelyn Underhill, *The Shape of the Liturgy* by Dom Gregory Dix, *Action in the Liturgy* by Walter Lowrie, *Eucharist and Sacrifice* by Gustaf Aulén, and the *Ecumenical Studies in Worship* (John Knox Press). A complete bibliography would have to include books on biblical theology along with the extensive literature on worship. Perhaps I should add that the primary source of this study is the Scriptures.

A personal word of appreciation is due to Robert C. Stanger, president emeritus of Elmhurst College. He not only offered helpful insights and critical comments to clear up some ambiguities in the text but also encouraged me with his enthusiastic endorsement of the project. The manuscript was typed by my former secretary, Laura Pickel. Gratefully I acknowledge the high quality of craftsmanship that has always been the hallmark of her work. While the manuscript was being reviewed by the publishers, two *Lord's Day Services* were released for study and experimentation. When in the light of these it seemed expedient to make revisions in several chapters, I called on Evelyn Schaudt, a former parishioner and good friend, to type the revised chapters. This she did with professional competence as a labor of love. My sincere thanks!

FREDERICK W. SCHROEDER

Elmhurst, Illinois

ACKNOWLEDGMENTS

The publisher acknowledges with appreciation permission to use copyrighted material from the following sources:

E. P. Dutton & Co., Inc., for the prayer by Archbishop Laud from *A Chain of Prayer* by Selina F. Fox.

Fortress Press for quotations from *Eucharist and Sacrifice* by Gustaf Aulén and *The Ecology of Faith* by Joseph Sittler.

Harper & Row, Publishers, for quotations from *Worship* by Evelyn Underhill and *Ways of Worship* by Pehr Edwall.

John Knox Press for quotations from *Worship and Congregation* by Wilhelm Hahn and *Essays on the Lord's Supper* by Oscar Cullmann and F. J. Leenhardt.

Macmillan Company for quotation from *Reality in Worship* by Willard Learoyd Sperry.

Oxford University Press for quotations from *Worship in Scripture and Tradition* edited by Massey H. Shepherd, Jr., and *Documents of the Christian Church* edited by Henry Bettenson.

Philosophical Library for quotations from *Action in the Liturgy* by Walter Lowrie.

Charles Scribner's Sons for quotations from *The Theology of the Sacraments* by Donald Baillie, *Prayers for Services* by Morgan Phelps Noyes, and *The Interpretation of History* by Paul Tillich.

The Westminster Press for quotations from *The Public Worship of God* by Henry Sloane Coffin and *Prophetic Realism and the Gospel* by John Wick Bowman.

CONTENTS

i · THE REDISCOVERY OF WORSHIP

Protestant Christianity has rediscovered the importance of worship in the life and work of the church. Such terms as liturgical renaissance, liturgical renewal, liturgical reform are common to the theological literature of our day. These terms do not have the same connotation in all circles. For example, the Jesuit scholar Michael J. Taylor in his survey of liturgical renewal within Protestant Christianity uses the term in the restricted sense of making it synonymous with sacramental renewal. His aim, as stated in the preface of *The Protestant Liturgical Renewal,* is "to discover whether or not American Protestants generally favor giving greater stress to the Lord's Supper in worship."[1]

By and large the term liturgical renewal or reform is used in the broader sense to designate the growing interest in public worship, particularly as it expresses itself in a more formal, not to say fixed, liturgy as contrasted to a relatively free or informal liturgy that allows for ad hoc alterations or additions as the mood of the minister might dictate or as the occasion might call for.

Most Protestant churches have become more liturgical in the sense that a given order of worship is followed every Sunday. This order may be simple or elaborate in the sense of being embellished with numerous choral and congregational responses; but regardless of how simple or elaborate it may be, it is nevertheless liturgical.

To attempt to draw a fine line of demarcation to differentiate between a liturgical and nonliturgical service of worship is next to impossible unless one limits a liturgical service to a liturgy that is fixed in both form and content. One may, however, distinguish between a more and a less liturgical form of worship. Aside from this, any order of worship that calls for congregational participation is necessarily a *leitourgia*—a work of the people. Liturgical renewal, then, as conceived of in this study, refers to the present trend of placing greater emphasis on worship per se, as distinguished from a one-sided emphasis on preaching. All things considered, this marks a wholesome advance.

There was a time when the average Protestant went to church to hear a sermon. He was led to believe that this was the primary if not the sole purpose of going to church. Moreover, preachers enamored with their eloquence and erudition, did not hesitate to ask the unchurched to come and hear them preach. That sort of blatant egotism has had its day. The invitation today is more apt to be: Come and worship. This is not to say that preaching has fallen into disrepute. In the Christian cultus, certainly in its Protestant form, preaching has an important place. Even as the reform movement within Catholicism is stressing the importance of preaching, so there is hope that the liturgical renaissance within Protestant Christianity may heighten its importance and indirectly contribute something to its improvement. If the liturgy exists to magnify the majesty and the mercy of God, then preaching—as one element of the liturgy—should be of a caliber that is in keeping with that high purpose. The sermon is not a display of the preacher's cleverness or competence; the sermon should set forth the unsearchable riches of the gospel.

From the very beginning Protestant Christianity exalted the preaching of the Word. The Word as proclaimed by sermon and sacrament has been the source of its vitality. Were it to turn its back upon a practice so central to its genius as preaching is, it would cease to be true to itself and impoverish its cultic life as well as forfeit its mission. Moreover, say what one will about the importance of worship—and this includes every phase and facet from invocation to benediction—the fact remains that the quality of preaching tends to make or break everything that transpires during the period of worship. When the sermon grips the heart and stimulates the mind, or when it is begotten and delivered as an act of worship, then everything else—the reading of the Scriptures, the prayers, the hymns of praise, and dedication—becomes more meaningful; worshipers leave the sanctuary refreshed. When the sermon is dull or irritates by its moralistic tone and content, the inspiration and encouragement, the comfort and commitment engendered by the Scriptures, prayers, and hymns are substantially diminished, if not completely destroyed. Good preaching—preaching which is simultaneously kerygmatic and charismatic—must always be an essential element of Christian worship.

However, the cultus of the church consists of more than preaching, preceded by what has even been called "an opening exercise," followed by an altar call. There are evidences of a refreshing emphasis on worship. The nature and art of worship have become a fertile field of theological inquiry. Ministers are experimenting with different forms of worship, sometimes blazing new trails, but more often merely harking back to some golden age when liturgical art was supposedly in full flower. The ecclesiastical year, hitherto almost unknown in some quarters, today is widely observed. The seasons from Advent through Trinity are appropriately designated with colored paraments;

even such names as Septuagesima and Quinquagesima—so difficult for the average layman to pronounce—have become familiar on the Sunday bulletin. Also the sacrament of Holy Communion is observed more frequently and faithfully than was customary some three or four decades ago.

Special attention is also being given to the pastoral or general prayer. Though largely free rather than fixed in the churches where extemporaneous prayers have long been the order of the day, they are now prepared with care both in regard to form and content. According to Willard L. Sperry an Australian churchman, when asked to give his impression of American church life, commented on the badness of our prayers. He had been depressed rather than impressed. This happened some thirty or forty years ago. It is doubtful whether any visiting churchman, though accustomed to a fixed liturgy, would have occasion to say that today. The aimless meanderings of pastoral prayers, with many exclamations of "Dear Lord," "O God," and the like, have all but disappeared from the scene. By and large the pastoral prayer of today is marked by orderliness in structure, chaste dignity in language, and an overall reverence consonant with man's approach to God. These qualities are the hallmark of public worship. What the psalmist spoke of as "the beauty of holiness," might well be said to characterize the Protestant cultus today.

THE FACTORS AND FORCES OF REFORM

What is the reason for the liturgical renaissance? That is a question well worth asking. A number of factors, converging more or less simultaneously, need to be considered. Although easily identified, they are not so easily listed in any order of priority, either as to impact or importance. Reaction is certainly one. First is the reaction against the informality that prevailed on the frontier. Worship on the frontier was extremely informal; inevitably so. A congregation of a dozen or more families, hastily assembled in a school or farmhouse when the circuit rider appeared upon the scene, could hardly be expected to follow an order of worship other than one improvised in keeping with the preacher's temperament and tradition. Obviously the kind of informality or formlessness that met the needs of people on the frontier will be deemed to be incongruous with the environment of a Gothic sanctuary on the city boulevard. Yet, as a matter of fact, with some modifications or, more likely, with some embellishments, the patterns of the frontier were perpetuated for quite some time in many urban communities. Within Methodism, for instance, as the members of the Order of St. Luke point out, the austere simplicity—not to say iconoclasm—of frontier puritanism and pietism is not in harmony with the denomination's rich liturgical heritage stemming from the Anglican Church.

There is also the reaction against the emotionalism associated with revival meetings. Emotional outbursts, sometimes bordering on hysteria, are looked upon with suspicion; certainly they are regarded to be in poor taste. Congregational participation, once largely a matter of enthusiastic singing accompanied by the clapping of hands and the stamping of feet and, not to be overlooked, occasional interjections of "Allelujah" and "Praise the Lord," has been channeled into responsive readings, litanies, and choral responses. Little by little the uncontrolled spontaneity of former days has given way to a planned orderliness. Paul, who insisted that "all things should be done decently and in order" (1 Cor. 14:40), would undoubtedly look with approval on the liturgical reform that is taking place but he might put in a plea for more spontaneity. It is worth noting that the cultic life of the Corinthian church was under review when the apostle coined this phrase that is frequently invoked in support of a carefully structured order of worship.

The liturgical renaissance is also a reaction against the exaggerated individualism which came to dominate the Protestant cultus under the influence of Pietism. Religion was thought to be a highly personal affair, largely confined to what a man did in and with his solitude. A worshiping congregation was conceived to be what might be called an aggregation of souls, each seeking salvation, rather than a corporate body firmly "joined and knit together" in the adoration and service of God for his unmerited mercies in Jesus Christ. Of the apostolic community it can be said that it was very much aware of being a koinonia, a fellowship uniquely bound together by its devotion to the crucified and risen Lord. Christian worship was never intended to be an individualistic enterprise, wallowing in a sea of subjectivism with the adoration of God subordinated to the edification of the self. Subjective worship might well produce a religious experience, even growth in the grace and the knowledge of the Lord Jesus Christ and assurance of salvation in the here and now as well as in the hereafter, but this is hardly in line with the oldest Christian tradition. It is not suggested here that the individual's needs and concerns are to be so completely subordinated to the corporate aspect of worship that his personal involvement becomes inconsequential. This is not the issue. All that is claimed here is that the liturgical renaissance is in part a reaction against the individualism, the emotionalism, and the informality that characterized Protestant worship in America for a long time.

If reaction is one factor to be taken into account by way of explaining the current interest in liturgical renewal, response to the ecumenical movement is another. Unlike the practice prevailing at many ecclesiastical gatherings where worship is often a sort of addendum to the agenda, worship has been given a place of importance at the great ecumenical conferences, notably at the assemblies of the World Council of Churches. Delegates praying together as well as working together have often discovered a oneness in worship that eluded them in discussions and debates around the conference table, in spite of considerable diversity in liturgical traditions. Unfortunately, the separate services of Holy Communion have laid bare a deep disunity which, however disturbing, has for that very reason lent a note of seriousness and urgency to the pursuit of liturgical renewal. This is particularly true in regard to worship at the Lord's table.

The rediscovery of Christian worship is one of the foremost blessings of the ecumenical movement. A Faith and Order study of the World Council of Churches dealing with worship declares, "It is heartening to realize that, at a time when Christians are perhaps more aware of the tragic estrangement of the world from the church than ever before, God is so plainly calling us to rediscover together the joy, the depth, and the power of Christian worship."[2]

The Faith and Order section initiated studies of worship such as those in *Ways of Worship*[3] and the series of *Ecumenical Studies in Worship*.[4] No longer is there a dearth of new literature touching on virtually every facet of worship. Worship has come into its own as a subject worthy of serious biblical and theological inquiry. The bearing this has on the cultic life of the church is becoming increasingly apparent.

Not to be overlooked, either, is the cross-fertilization of liturgical traditions, which the ecumenical movement has brought about. Distinctive denominational patterns of worship, which prevailed for a long time, are hardly discernible anymore. It has become difficult—if not impossible—to distinguish among a typical Presbyterian, Congregational, Baptist, or Methodist liturgical pattern. So widespread has been the interaction and interchange within Protestant Christianity that apart from the name of the church and the denominational imprimatur in the hymnal, one is hard pressed to determine a congregation's affiliation by its form of worship. Indeed, one is apt to find as many liturgical differences within each household of faith as there are differences between the major Protestant bodies. Perhaps the only exceptions to this rule are Episcopalians and Lutherans who by tradition have followed a fixed liturgy.

However, it should also be noted that what appears to be cross-fertilization in matters of worship may in some instances be nothing other than borrowing from the past or conforming to the trend of the times. Cultus reform is in the ecclesiastical air of our time. Liturgical alterations and embellishments are the order of the day. It would be strange indeed if the pressure to conform—so pervasive and powerful in matters of opinion and style—did not assert itself in the church as well. By way of illustration, one need only recall that until rather recently Gothic architecture in some form or other was the vogue. Today, relatively few Gothic churches are being built. One of the reasons for the shift to modern forms of architecture is financial. The cost of a Gothic structure has become well-nigh prohibitive. But the interior arrangement of the altar-centered chancel—so much a part of the Gothic period—appears to be more firmly entrenched than ever. To what extent this is due to conformity is hard to say. One suspects, however, that to a large degree it is dictated by the liturgical renaissance that has made Protestants very altar-conscious. To propose a pulpit-centered sanctuary with a free-standing communion table beneath it or in front of it to symbolize the unity of Word and sacrament, as was customary in the Reformed tradition, is to defy what is considered to be liturgically correct.

Statistics proving the pressure of cultus conformity are difficult to assemble. There appears to be an uneasy feeling abroad that unless the liturgy is updated to include litanies, chants, and responses—with various symbolical movements and postures—one is not liturgically au courant. When the question is raised as to why more ritualism has been introduced, the answer is apt to be: this is the way it is done in other churches of the city or denomination, or, this is what people like and want. Not theology, not even tradition, but vogue or popular demand is the determining factor.

Often aesthetic and psychological factors appear to receive more consideration than theological principles. Changes are introduced because they have eye appeal or are presumed to be effective. It is said that people want color and drama such as the Roman mass provides. The mass is indeed colorful, even somewhat mysterious. The genuflections of the priest beget a sense of awe; his movements and chants are impressive. The worshiper may not always understand just what is being done, but he can see and hear that something is actually happening. He is aware that in some way the drama of the atonement is being reenacted.

Protestant Christianity has nothing to match this unless it be ceremonial pomp and pageantry gratuitously injected. And sometimes this is done. The procession, intended to provide an orderly entrance for the choir as well as to lift and lead the congregation in adoration and praise, becomes a parade. A theological justification for acolytes and altar candles might be hard to come by, but the ceremony of lighting and extinguishing the candles, executed with a kind of solemn dignity, is impressive. The pulpit robe, symbolizing the teaching ministry and incidentally covering up sartorial elegance or angular individuality, is often hidden today under chasuble, alb, and stole. This has been called "putting religion back in Sunday clothes." It can also be a subtle way of introducing sacerdotal elements of dubious validity.

These and other externals of liturgical practice are matters of taste that could be passed up without further comment. Tastes, according to an old Latin saying, are not to be disputed. But when the shape of the liturgy is determined to give it dramatic appeal, there is a need to be on guard lest this leads to sterile ritualism or encourages spectatorship. One of the criticisms leveled against the mass from within Catholicism as well as from without, has to do with this very issue. With justification it has been claimed that the mass encourages worshipers to be spectators. A number of reform measures have been taken to correct this situation. Bishops have been given authority to have a portion of the mass read in the vernacular wherever that is desired. This will make for a more meaningful participation. This same concern for participation also underlies the current trend to move the altar from the wall, so that in effect it becomes a table around which priest and people may gather for the sacrament. The reform movement within Catholicism clearly recognizes that participation, not observation, is of the very essence of worship.

To say that participation is of the very essence of worship is not to say that liturgy and drama are necessarily antithetical. Good drama invites participation. To witness a tragedy on the stage is a moving experience. Spectators become involved to the point of suffering vicariously. If one purpose of the liturgy is that of setting forth the mighty deeds of God in history, its other purpose is to enlist the worshiper in the divine action. One would not want to deny that this is the intent of the mass, which is basically a reenactment or representation of the atonement. The same holds true of the Orthodox liturgy, which celebrates the mystery of the incarnation. Protestant liturgies—not as restricted in scope and content—also recall God's deeds in both nature and history through the media of scripture, creeds, hymns, prayers, and sermon. The sacrament of the Lord's Supper does this in a very special way as far as the atonement is concerned. For whether the Lord's Supper is conceived of as a mystical representation of Christ's atoning death on the cross or whether it is observed simply in remembrance of him without any mystical overtones, it unmistakably sets forth the mercy of God. Unless one comes to the Lord's table as a matter of habit or in a perfunctory manner, one must of necessity remember "how hard it was for our Savior to bear our sins and the sins of the whole world . . . by offering up his life and shedding his blood."[5]

HAZARDS OF THE LITURGICAL RENAISSANCE

Reference has already been made to certain hazards brought to the fore by the liturgical renaissance. A further word on this matter may be in order. There is first of all the danger of destroying the blush and bloom of worship when it is subjected to critical analysis. An act so personal tends to lose some of its luster in the process of careful examination. Worship is an act of spontaneous adoration rather than an object about which one theologizes or psychologizes. The beauty and fragrance of a rose are destroyed when a scientist takes that rose into the laboratory to dissect and analyze its structure under a microscope or to capture its fragrance in a test tube. Obviously it is good to know the component elements of a rose, but such knowledge is a poor substitute for a rose. Similarly, a study of worship yields many valuable insights, but all things considered, it is better to worship in spirit and in truth than to be liturgically correct—if one may speak of liturgical correctness. Spirit is more important than form.

Isaiah's vision in the temple in the year that King Uzziah died might be cited as a classic example of the movement of worship (Isa. 6:8). According to the prophet's own words he experienced an overpowering awareness of the majesty of God; next came a deep sense of his unworthiness; and then when his sin had been forgiven he was ready to say: "Here am I! Send me." These three moods describe what takes place when man really and truly worships. Hence, there is considerable merit in shaping the liturgy in such a way that the upward look will lead to the inward look, and the two will beget the outward look. Yet it should be recognized that the warmth and vitality of worship cannot be guaranteed by adopting this or any other formula. To become too conscious of the process is to run the risk of losing the glow and the glory of worship.

Now the shaping of the liturgy is in the first instance limited to liturgiologists. Not completely, however; certainly not when they are officially commissioned to produce an order of worship for general use throughout a given denomination. *The Service for the Lord's Day*[6] and *The Lord's Day Service*,[7] both published in 1964, the former jointly by Presbyterian bodies and the latter by the United Church of Christ, are a case in point. Ministers and members of congregations are urged to study these books and to be governed by them as much as possible. Reference to these two orders of worship suggest that what liturgiologists design around the conference table ultimately involves all congregations where the new order is introduced.

Since the cultic life of the church tends to be conservative, in the sense of holding fast to treasured customs, a new order of worship is not apt to meet with immediate approval, especially if the suggested order departs radically from the one that has served a congregation over a long period of time. Moreover, an element of coercion is apt to enter in even though there is no attempt to force congregations to follow the prescribed form. Whether intentional or not, a liturgy invested with a quasi-official imprimatur tends to place freedom of worship in jeopardy. More than that, many of the faithful become troubled and disturbed, wondering whether they and their forefathers have perchance worshiped in ignorance these many years and centuries. This could easily lead to an unsettling of the faith of the saints at a point where they are least in need of being unsettled.

One has reason to be grateful for every endeavor made to set up an order that enables people to participate freely and reverently in the act of worship. Nevertheless, the church must be on guard lest freedom give way to rigidity and spontaneity be sacrificed for cultic regularity. This caveat is prompted by the observation that from those in the forefront of liturgical reform there emanates a persistent and vigorous emphasis that the officially approved liturgy be followed in all churches. Repeatedly Protestant Christianity has been under the necessity of emancipating itself from creedal conformity. Is it now to become fettered by a cultic rigidity?

It is the glory of the Protestant faith, largely because of its many varieties, that it has fostered freedom of worship. Admittedly, this has not been an unmixed blessing. Vagaries of one kind or another are so well-known that they need not be cataloged. Perhaps there are few ministers in the free church tradition who have not in one way or another experimented with the liturgy, and sometimes not very wisely. For example, the intent or movement of worship is sometimes spelled out in the order by such neatly schematized captions as adoration, confession, instruction, and consecration. One may well ask whether worship can be so facilely structured that it will naturally fall into such a pattern. The moods and movements of the human spirit do not always conform to a predetermined scheme. "The wind blows where it wills, and you hear the sound of it, but you do not know whence it comes or whither it goes; so it is with every one who is born of the Spirit" (John 3:8). These words of Jesus are as pertinent in describing the nuances of worship as they are in setting forth the mystery of being born anew. Man's worship can be directed but it cannot be put into a straightjacket. Instead of telling the worshiper in advance what spiritual posture he is to take at a particular point in the service—awe, gratitude, humility, or dedication— it is better to let the movement of the liturgy speak for itself.

The captions just mentioned have the added liability that they do not always coincide with what is called for. The preaching of the Word cannot always be followed appropriately with a hymn of consecration. There are times when the sermon is more properly followed with a hymn of praise for God's unmerited mercies, or, if the message has pricked the heart, a hymn of penitence may be very much in order. Therefore, the pattern suggested by captions, however well-intended, is too inflexible to be useful.

What may be an even greater liability of any such schematization is the fact that it tends to get in the way of what, for want of a better term, may be called the organic oneness of worship. Moods or attitudes of adoration, confession, petition, thanksgiving, intercession, and consecration may occur more or less simultaneously; they also occur in an unpredictable order. There is an alternation of mood that cannot be predetermined. And the freedom of the Spirit ought not to be inhibited by unnecessary man-made rubrics. The free movement of the Spirit is paramount.

An unalterable, fixed liturgy is somewhat presumptuous. There is no one form for which finality can be claimed. Ecclesiologically speaking, it is generally agreed that the New Testament does not contain a blueprint as to whether the episcopal, the presbyterial, or the congregational structure is of the very esse of the church. With equal conviction it can be said that the New Testament contains no apostolic liturgy that embodies the very esse of Christian worship. We refer to the New Testament not to find a pattern of worship but to discover the spirit and theological principles that the liturgy of the church should embody. Not tradition but theology is definitive for determining the shape of the liturgy.

PRIORITY OF THEOLOGICAL PRINCIPLES

Lest Protestant Christianity turn its back on its legacy of faith stemming from the prophetic and apostolic tradition via the Reformation, it is imperative that the theological presuppositions of worship be kept clearly in view. This is not to say that tradition should be ignored. There is much that can be learned from the liturgies of the past. But an uncritical adoption or adaptation of the liturgical classics of another day without regard to their theological implications is unwarranted. A meaningful liturgy must not only be consonant with what the church believes but also it must grow out of the life of the worshiping community in order to speak to this community. A liturgy that grew out of the life of the church in the fifth or fifteenth century, however meaningful then, may not speak at all to men and women of the twentieth century. Yet there is a marked tendency to look to the past and to borrow from the past.

Two examples of this tendency come to mind. Paul Tillich tells of having been a member of a small group that was organized in Germany in the 1920's to work together to overcome what he speaks of as "the horrors of the nineteenth-century liturgies and all their sentimental nonsense." No specifics are given. However, what is significant is the fact that the group became divided. Some sought to rediscover the liturgical riches of the past, whereas others, of whom he was one, realized that the needs of twentieth-century workers and intellectuals are not apt to be met by fourth- or fifth-century liturgies. The antiquarians, as Tillich calls them, were victorious but at the cost of further alienating the church from the very people it wanted to serve.[8]

Another example is that of the Church of South India. In a series of ecumenical studies in worship, T. S. Barrett admits that "the liturgical forms in use in South India, whether pre-union or post-union, are for the most part imported from the West, and that even those elements in them which have had their birth in India show marked signs of Western influence."[9] The Western influence in this instance is *The Book of Common Prayer*. Although this service book has stood the test of time remarkably well, it is questionable whether its underlying modes of thought are as meaningful in the Orient as they are in the land of their origin.

When the shape of the liturgy is determined by older patterns, the mistake is sometimes made of not taking the entire cultus of the church into consideration. Someone once said that the chief liability of "the old-time religion" which was good enough for father, mother, and other worthy forebears, is that it is not old enough. It does not go back to the prophets and apostles for its precepts and examples, not even to the Reformers. Thus it is found wanting in its depth and breadth of outlook. James H. Nichols entitled his recent critique of the new Presbyterian liturgy "Is the New 'Service' Reformed?"[10] In his judgment the proposed service does not do justice to the elements of repentance, reverence, and holy awe that were basic in Calvin's understanding of the Eucharist. A bird's-eye view of present liturgical tendencies leads one to ask whether the full sweep of liturgical history is taken sufficiently into account, notably its beginnings in apostolic times when simplicity and spontaneity constituted the hallmark of worship.

Simplicity is not very pronounced in recent liturgical products. And, in the words of Seward Hiltner, they concede only "a smidgen to spontaneity." Obviously it is neither possible nor desirable to restore the pattern of worship that prevailed in New Testament times. In the first place, the New Testament does not provide us with a clearly defined form of worship. The Christian cultus was still very fluid in the apostolic period. Very likely the form of worship varied somewhat from one community to another. In regard to the Eucharist, for instance, at least two traditions can be traced back to early times. Even if it would be possible to restore an apostolic form of worship, no useful purpose would be served in doing so. The culture and the customs, the outlook and the expectations of the twentieth century are so radically different from those of the first, that the liturgical practices of that day have little more than historical interest today. But in matters of theology the New Testament is our primary source. Unless the cultus of the church is rooted in and grounded on theological principles that are biblically sound it will be found wanting.

Will Herberg has made the claim that "American religion is nontheological and nonliturgical."[11] Whether this is as true today as it was three or more decades ago is debatable. What should be of concern, however, is whether American religion is becoming more liturgical—which it unquestionably is—before or without becoming more theological. In the interest of fostering purity in the cultus of the church, theological literacy should precede liturgical renewal or reform. For as the Roman Catholic theologian Gustave Weigel pointed out in his foreword to Michael Taylor's *Protestant Liturgical Renewal* "theology shapes the liturgy and the liturgy in turn shapes theology."[12] When the latter is the case, the resulting liturgy is apt to be as questionable as the theology it begets is heretical.

The Roman mass is a good example. Though it may be impossible to establish beyond all shadow of doubt which came first —theology or liturgy—the probability is that the liturgy of the mass did much by way of shaping the theology of the church. Well-known is the fact that the simple celebration of the Eucharist in New Testament times became overlaid with elaborate sacerdotal elements that stemmed in part from the priestly tradition of Judaism and in part from the mystery religions of the East. Those elements became firmly entrenched in the liturgical practice of the church eventuating finally in an official theology. At the Council of Trent the Roman Church declared: "Since in this divine sacrifice which is performed in the mass, that same Christ is contained in a bloodless sacrifice who on the altar of the cross once offered himself with the shedding of his blood: the holy synod teaches that this sacrifice is truly propitiatory."[13] Even though the sharp edge of this doctrine of reenactment is being blunted by those Roman Catholic theologians who prefer to speak of representation instead of reenactment, the official theology of the Roman Church remains unchanged.

To be sure, there is no guarantee that all is necessarily well when theology shapes the liturgy, for theology is just as much subject to error as liturgy. Nevertheless, what is believed should precede and inform the cultic life of the church. When what is believed is firmly grounded in the Scriptures the resulting liturgy will be at least theologically sound, though it might possibly lack aesthetic appeal. The Reformers, for instance, did not hesitate to introduce radical changes in worship because they found some of the assumptions underlying the mass to be unbiblical. It is possible that some people deemed the Zwinglian form of worship to be extremely austere; by most standards it still is to this day.

Though Luther was not as radical in the matters of worship that were not strictly prohibited by scripture, his *Deutsche Messe* was a sacramental, not a sacrificial rite. What had been a sacrifice offered to God to atone for sin became a sacrifice of praise and thanksgiving offered in acknowledgment of divine grace already received. Furthermore, by urging that the altar be moved from the wall to permit the celebrant to face the people, which was traditional in the Western church for almost the first thousand years of its history, Luther recaptured for the Eucharist the New Testament concept of a Lord's table around which the faithful could gather to break the bread and drink of the cup "in remembrance of him."

All this points up how important theology is for liturgy. Because the worship of the church must be consonant with what the church believes about God and his mighty deeds in history, the concern of this book is basically theological. What the church believes grows out of God's self-revelation in the course of history—particularly from the revelation given to the prophets and apostles of old—and even more specifically out of his self-disclosure in Jesus Christ, who "reflects the glory of God and bears the very stamp of his nature" (Heb. 1:3).

ii · THE THEOCENTRIC
NATURE OF WORSHIP

Worship has been variously defined. In the broadest sense, worship is simply the recognition of worth; in the religious sense, it means rendering homage to a deity in recognition of his worth. Evelyn Underhill defines Christian worship as "the total adoring response of man to the one Eternal God self-revealed in time."[1] Henry Sloane Coffin speaks of worship as "the awed and glad spontaneous response of the spirit of man confronted by the God of Christian revelation—the God of creation and redemption."[2] Speaking for the Theological Commission of Faith and Order, Pehr Edwall declares worship to be "the concentration of all faculties on corporate self-giving to God in response to his love and in praise of his glory."[3]

These definitions have one thing in common—they emphasize the theocentric character of worship. To quote Evelyn Underhill again, "worship . . . always means God and the priority of God."[4] The theocentric nature of worship is pronounced and most effectively portrayed in Psalm 8:1 where the psalmist exults: "O Lord, our Lord, how majestic is thy name in all the earth." Said another psalmist: "Great is the Lord and greatly to be praised" (Ps. 48:1). Not only did Israel's poets call upon their fellowmen to acknowledge Yahweh's greatness but also at least one of their number summoned himself to be faithful in doing so. "Bless the Lord, O my soul," exclaims the author of Psalm 103:1. In another psalm the heavens are spoken of as "telling the glory of God" (Ps. 19:1); and in still another, heavenly beings are invited to "ascribe to the Lord the glory of his name; [to] worship the Lord in holy array" (Ps. 29:2).

Contrary to what is commonly assumed, the theocentric manner of worship has little if anything to do with the instruction and edification of the worshiper. In an essay on "Worship and Ethics in Theology," Elmer J. F. Arndt stated the issue succinctly in one sentence: "When worship is prized because of the satisfaction it offers or directed to the arousal and stimulation of experiences in worshipers, worship ceases to be the expression of faith and becomes the expression of unfaith."[5] "Divine service," writes Walter Lowrie, "is an action which we perform in God's honor. It is not worship if it is performed deliberately with a view to our own interest, whether as a meritorious work or for our spiritual edification."[6] Worship at its highest and best is the act of giving to God the honor and glory that are his due, without regard to any personal satisfaction or benefit accruing from the act of adoration. It would be a mistake, however, to assume that people always reach this high level of self-immolation in the act of worship. Human need in some form or other does enter the picture, even if it be no other need than the need to worship; that is, the need to relate oneself to God.

Job's cry, "Oh, that I knew where I might find him, that I might come even to his seat!" (Job 23:3), and the psalmist's yearning, "My soul thirsts for God, for the living God" (Ps. 42:2), are expressions of this need. They are as genuine acts of worship as the more common declarations of praise and adoration found throughout the Psalter. Some element of true worship that will give life meaning and purpose may be at hand even when men are basically concerned about peace of mind or in search of a mountaintop experience. Purists in matters of worship, especially those who regard worship primarily in terms of recapitulating the mighty deeds of God in Christ, might disagree; but one can easily draw the boundary lines too narrow and too tight, thereby reducing worship to an esoteric cult reserved for the spiritually enlightened and elite.

To mention another caveat, it is said that worship is God-initiated. An Old Testament psalmist seems to be saying this when in distress he declares: "Thou hast said, 'Seek ye my face.' My heart says to thee, 'Thy face, Lord, do I seek'" (Ps. 27:8). Wilhelm Hahn of Heidelberg contends that "worship is first and foremost God's service to us. . . . Our activity in worship can be nothing other than reaction and response, the consequence of God's activity."[7] But this seems to be overstating the case. It is true that we would scarcely be seeking God unless he had first sought us, but if this principle is applied too rigorously, it minimizes man's responsibility in order to magnify God's initiative. One is moved to ask: Is God honored when man, made in his image and endowed with the freedom and responsibility to choose, is reduced to a state of waiting helplessly until God takes the initiative? If it is proper to speak of God's initiating the act of worship, then such act can be identified with the capacity and the need for worship with which man is endowed.

WORSHIP AS RECOGNITION AND RESPONSE

The definitions of worship cited in the introductory paragraph have this in common—paramount is the recognition of God in his unshared sovereignty, in his holy love, in his infinite grace and mercy. Worship is the act of acknowledging that God is God, that he alone is worthy of man's highest praise and deepest loyalty. The first commandment puts this into focus when it declares: "You shall have no other gods before me" (Exod. 20:3). This demand is not easily met. Even in moments set aside for the celebration of God's presence and power, man tends to vacillate between the God who, as the summum bonum, is beyond all human understanding and some lesser good, be that a person or a possession elevated to the place of adoration that should be reserved for God.

The recognition of God as supremely worthful, as "the ultimate basis of reliance," to use a phrase of Bishop James Pike, is made possible only because of God's action. As pure being, however, God is beyond man's comprehension. God is known only by what God does. God has revealed himself as Creator, Redeemer, and sanctifying Spirit. His self-disclosure is not all of one kind or of one time and place. It is true that his self-disclosure as Redeemer in Jesus Christ is central and makes for a more meaningful understanding of his revelation as Creator and Holy Spirit.

The bearing this has on worship is considerable. Specifically this means that the Christian Event—the birth, life, death, and resurrection of Jesus Christ—is the focal point of Christian worship. "We cannot discuss worship as though we were still in the old aeon, on the other side of Pentecost and the resurrection," wrote Joseph Sittler in an article prepared for the Faith and Order Commission on Worship.[8] It is a fact of history that over the centuries since Christ's birth, Christian worship has not been so completely focused on the Christian Event that other aspects of God's self-revelation have been overlooked. The Eastern Orthodox liturgy celebrating the incarnation and the Roman mass concentrating on the atonement might possibly be considered exceptions to the overall practice that has prevailed in Christendom from the beginning.

It is important to remember that Christian worship has its

roots in Hebrew worship, particularly in synagogue worship. The primitive church leaned heavily on the Old Testament for scripture and hymnody, and to this day the church borrows extensively from the liturgical resources of the psalter. And rightly so. Just as the Hebrew prophets offer valuable insights for Christian social action, so the psalmists provide helpful treasures for Christian worship. Biblical scholarship in these days is rightfully emphasizing the unity of the Old and New Testaments. The God of the patriarchs and the prophets is the God and Father of our Lord Jesus Christ. Whatever dissimilarity or discontinuity there may seem to be between the two testaments is in our understanding of God's action, not in any change in God's nature. God is and always has been the same. Calvary did not change anything in the character of God, for it was God in Christ "reconciling the world to himself."

Christian worship must aim to give recognition to God for all of his mighty and merciful deeds. The cause of true worship is not served when divine providence, divine sovereignty, divine judgment are treated as being only ancillary to his divine mercy as revealed in Jesus Christ. The liturgy of the church, no less than the preaching of the word, needs to be informed by what the apostle Paul called the whole counsel of God. Fortunately, the hymns of the church embody this principle to a marked degree. Along with hymns celebrating the incarnation and recalling the atonement and the resurrection, the average church hymnal contains a wide variety of hymns, ranging from those extolling God's sovereignty and providence to the church's responsibility to proclaim the gospel and to work for justice and brotherhood. What a pity that too often many of these great treasures of the Christian faith are seldom employed in the worship of God. Nevertheless, the fact remains that a wide selection of hymns in regard to content is available. This bears witness that worship in the Protestant tradition seeks to incorporate not only every facet of divine self-disclosure but also every avenue and aspect of man's responsibility to serve God and magnify his name.

If *recognition* is the word that has predominated in our discussion up to this point, *response* must now be added as its correlative. Response and recognition go together. Response runs the whole gamut of attitudes and actions from awe, gratitude, joy, and humility to obedience, surrender, and sacrifice. When man really worships, he responds with an attitude commensurate with the depth of his appreciation. Of a lover it is sometimes said that he worships the very ground on which his beloved walks. If that sounds a bit sacrilegious, let it be clearly understood that the phrase is intended to say no more than to express the lover's complete dedication, complete commitment—the kind of commitment that worship calls for. And when love runs deep, many ways are found to express it. Sometimes it is done in a declaration couched in terms of endearment, sometimes by a gift, sometimes by a fond embrace, or possibly by nothing more dramatic than an overarching concern and thoughtfulness. The recognition of God's inestimable greatness and goodness, just as a man's love for a woman, calls for a response commensurate with the place God has in life or, more correctly stated, with the place God ought to have in life.

What, then, is the nature of this response? Adoration is the dominant motif found in the psalter. Whether the psalmists spoke for Israel or only for themselves is hard to say, but the adoration of God was their chief concern and their highest joy. Their lyrical product anticipated the Westminster Catechism's declaration that "man's chief end is to glorify God and to enjoy him forever." The hymns of praise and adoration, even the laments that flowed from the hearts and minds of the Hebrew poets, testify unmistakably that they considered the worship of the Lord of hosts to be a high privilege and a joyous affair. "I was glad when they said to me, 'Let us go to the house of the Lord!'"

one of their number exclaimed. The tenor of this poem found in Psalm 122:1 suggests that he shouted it from the housetops. Worship was no unpleasant chore as far as he was concerned. If his testimony is at all typical, one can conclude that Hebrew worship was marked by an exuberance that is unique. Such phrases as "sing to the Lord" (Exod. 15:21), "enter his gates with thanksgiving, and his courts with praise" (Ps. 100:4), and "make a joyful noise to the rock of our salvation" (Ps. 95:1) say all that needs to be said on that score.

Adoration expressed only in words, whether spoken or sung, can be grossly inadequate. Appropriately enough, the psalmists were not content simply to extol God with hymns of praise and thanksgiving; they enjoined worshipers to "bring an offering, and come into his courts" (Ps. 96:8).

In matters of public worship the psalmists appear to have bridged the gap between the austerity of prophetic religion and the lush ceremonialism of priestly religion. If there was any tendency in Israel to appear before the Lord with empty hands, the temple cult was designed to discourage and counteract it. Trespass offerings and thank offerings, to mention just these two, were expected of every descendant of Abraham. Whatever questions might be raised about the sacrificial cult enshrined in the temple, its underlying principle was sound. The act of worship without an offering of substance or the surrender of self falls short of being an adequate response. "Worship," according to Evelyn Underhill, "is summed up in sacrifice."[9]

In point of time, tangible offerings preceded songs and ceremonies. It is recorded that Cain and Abel brought the firstfruits of field and flock. Worship was as simple as that. This story harks back to the prehistorical past and must not be used as a proof text. It may, however, be regarded as a fairly typical description of primitive worship in general. With the rise of culture, notably with the development of the fine arts, rituals, and incantations, hymnody came to have a place along with offerings and oblations. Psalm 116 has a good blending of song and sacrifice as the poet, fitting his words to the act, declares: "I will offer to thee the sacrifice of thanksgiving and call on the name of the Lord. I will pay my vows to the Lord in the presence of all his people, in the courts of the house of the Lord" (Ps. 116:17-19). In due time words of penitence and praise, either spoken or sung, gradually replaced the various kinds of animal sacrifices. In synagogue worship, for instance, the prayer of penitence became a substitute for the sin offering that was formerly brought to the temple and sacrificed on the altar. Nevertheless, synagogue worship was not void of every trace of substantive offerings.

Worship cannot be considered complete unless it expresses itself in something more substantial than a religious posture or a liturgical ceremony. Without an offering of substance or the surrender of self, worship falls short of being an adequate response to the Lord who spared not his own Son. By and large, this is universally recognized. If it were not so, ornate temples, majestic cathedrals, beautiful shrines and churches would never have been built. It is amazing how generously men have given of their time, talent, and substance to magnify the name of the Lord in massive, impressive, artistic structures of stone and steel, stained glass, and beautifully carved wood. Few, if any, utilitarian considerations seem to have entered the picture when the great cathedrals of Europe were built. Granted that those cathedrals reflect in part the pride and the vanity of man, nevertheless, they are to be viewed primarily as man's attempt to glorify God. Seen from this perspective, cathedrals and sanctuaries are priceless monuments of man's response to the Creator of all things.

An offering of substance, such as a lamb or a bullock in ancient times or money today, is not necessarily an act of true worship. Instead of being an act of worship, giving of one's substance can be a substitute for the self-giving or self-surrender for which it is meant. The Hebrew prophets, notably Isaiah and Micah, saw the hollowness of what was presumed to be worship. Isaiah's scathing denunciation of the temple cult is equaled only by the "woe-to-you" thunderbolts hurled at the scribes and Pharisees by Jesus. Cried the prophet in words from the lips of Yahweh: "What to me is the multitude of your sacrifices? . . . I have had enough of burnt offerings of rams and the fat of fed beasts. . . . When you come to appear before me, who requires of you this trampling of my courts? Bring no more vain offerings; incense is an abomination to me" (Isa. 1:11-13).

What distressed Isaiah along with Micah, Amos, and Hosea was not merely the fact that burnt offerings and solemn assemblies had become a substitute for true worship, but that it became a profanation of God. He had become what God is not—a deity demanding sacrifices and adulations. God is not a Lord who wants *things*: lambs, goats, ceremonial pomp and pageantry, stocks and bonds or their cash equivalent. God wants something far more radical than any and all material gifts. He desires a humble spirit, a contrite heart, a relationship of love and trust and obedience. This is the unanimous testimony of the Hebrew prophets. Sacrifices from field and flock are acceptable only when they express commitment; otherwise they are meaningless. The Creator of the universe, as a psalmist pointed out, has no need of things, for all things are his already: "For every beast of the forest is mine, the cattle on a thousand hills . . . the world and all that is in it is mine" (Ps. 50:10, 12).

Worship must be in harmony with the character of God. If God is a celestial potentate, capricious and vainglorious, that calls for one kind of response; but if God is as he is seen in the face of Jesus Christ, righteous and compassionate, an entirely different kind of response is needed. This means that an offering of substance, however generous, is not in itself a guarantee of true worship.

Worship can be genuine, whether verbalized or ceremonialized, when it is an act of self-giving. "The gift without the giver is bare,"[10] in worship no less than in charity. Was it not Isaiah's complaint that his people honored God with their lips only while their hearts were far removed? The hiatus between heart and hand, between profession and performance, was too obvious to go unnoticed. This situation is by no means confined to one race or religion. It is a universal and a perennial failing. How urgent, therefore, to heed the words of the apostle Paul: "I appeal to you, therefore, brethren, by the mercies of God to present your bodies a living sacrifice, holy and acceptable to God, which is your spiritual worship" (Rom. 12:1). A living sacrifice is not one specific act but rather an ongoing, continuous worship. And when the apostle speaks of presenting "your bodies," he is calling for the commitment of the whole person. This he calls "spiritual worship," or, as the older translations rendered it, "reasonable service" or "spiritual service."

It is worth noting that these slightly different translations suggest that worship and service are very much one and the same. To us these words denote different functions; apparently the New Testament writers made no such sharp distinction. To worship God is to serve God, and to serve is to worship. One without the other is incomplete. Both facets are uniquely caught up in the German word for worship. A Sunday service of worship is called a *Gottesdienst;* literally, a God-service. Response to God in contemplating his greatness and goodness, his unfathomable mystery, and his infinite mercy can be one form of service. Psalm 139 is a good example. Here was a man so overwhelmed by the omniscience and omnipresence of the Eternal that he was moved with awe and ecstasy. On the other hand, God is served, as James tells us, by visiting "orphans and widows in their affliction" (Jas. 1:27); that is, by service rendered in his name. And that is worship too.

Cultus and conduct belong together. If one had to choose between the two, conduct would come first, for "to obey is better
than sacrifice," as Samuel said by way of rebuking King Saul for
having confiscated the cattle and sheep of the defeated enemy
on the pretext of offering them as a sacrifice of thanksgiving for
victory (1 Sam. 15:22). Centuries later Hosea, speaking for the
Lord, said the same thing in slightly different words: "For I
desire steadfast love and not sacrifice, the knowledge of God,
rather than burnt offerings" (Hos. 6:6).

Worship as Relationship and Renewal

Christian worship, to repeat, is theocentric. It is man's recognition of God and his awed and joyful response to God. Yet worship is not a street with one-way traffic only. Its movement is
not solely from man toward God; simultaneously there is a
movement from God toward man. Two words that might be
used to describe this aspect of worship are relationship and
renewal. Henry Sloane Coffin uses the word communion, and
declares this to be the high point of worship.[11] What begins as an
act of adoration leads to a moment when the worshiper, seeking
to be aware of God, knows that he is apprehended by God and
is thereby inwardly renewed. "Behold this has touched your
lips," said the seraphim with a burning coal in his hand, "your
guilt is taken away, and your sin is forgiven" (Isa. 6:7). The
Quaker philosopher Rufus Jones spoke of worship as a double
search, meaning that it is at one and the same time man's search
for God and God's search for man.

Evelyn Underhill, though stressing that "not man's needs and
wishes, but God's presence and incitement" evoke worship,
nevertheless admits that "from first to last self-regarding elements are mixed up with human worship."[12] It could hardly be
otherwise, for man is made in the image of God. Augustine declared that our hearts are restless until they find their rest in

God. "Deep calls to deep" not only "at the thunder of thy cataracts" (Ps. 42:7), but in the quiet moments of life as well when no crisis is at hand. This is to say that man is moved to worship not only because of some pressing need for security or deliverance but also because of what he is: a "worshiping animal," as he has been called.

The quest for God that cries out "When shall I come and behold the face of God?" (Ps. 42:2) is in some sense self-regarding. God is being sought not only for his own sake but also for the seeker's own sake. Man seeks this relationship to find what might be called self-fulfillment. There is no reason to regard this as a debased or debasing facet of worship, certainly not if worship is in a real sense a divine-human encounter. "In all sympathetic intercourse between persons there is," what Dr. Coffin calls, "a communication or conveyance of selves."[13] In worship, man speaks to God and God to man. The latter receives far too little attention. We are so busy talking to God, laying before him our various needs and concerns, that our hearts are not attuned to hear his voice. Be that as it may, apprehending God and being apprehended by God are two sides of the same coin, and they occur more or less simultaneously.

If worship means the offering of ourselves to God, it follows that in this act we present to him our penitence for our short-comings and our aspirations for a better life, along with our praise and thanksgiving for favors and mercies already received. Self-regarding elements of this nature are not necessarily a perversion of worship. Would it not be an affront to the God of Christian revelation to say that the needs of his children are of no concern to him? Jesus said: "Ask, and it will be given you; seek, and you will find; knock, and it will be opened to you" (Matt. 7:7). To be sure, this refers specifically to prayer; and prayer and worship are not quite synonymous. Theoretically, the latter could be said to be unalloyed adoration. But who can draw a sharp line to determine where worship becomes prayer and prayer becomes worship? There is an interrelatedness here that cannot be separated without doing violence to one or the other.

This should not blind us to the fact that worship does tend to become bogged down in the quest for self-fulfillment. However, the perversion of that which is valid in the I-Thou relationship, in the divine-human encounter, or in the "mystic sweet communion" of spirit with Spirit, must not lead us to throw the baby out with the bath. Pehr Edwall sounds a note of caution that we ignore at our peril. "There is danger," he writes, "that some advocates of the liturgical movement might so emphasize the aspect of oblation that all concern for the edification of the worshiper would disappear."[14] Not to be overlooked is the fact that the Westminster declaration contains a double emphasis. "Man's chief end is to glorify God, *and enjoy him forever*" (italics added). The glorification of God and man's enjoyment of God are not incompatible or contradictory. Enjoyment, or call it edification, is an inherent element in and a legitimate aspect of worship. Wilhelm Hahn cites the apostle Paul (1 Cor. 14:26) in support of his claim "that everything in the worship of the community must be done with a view to the edification of the community."[15]

The issue comes into sharp focus when Roman Catholic worship is compared with Protestant worship. The former has been characterized as objective worship in its purest form for the reason that very little, if any, attention is given to the worshiper. Every word that is spoken, every chant that is heard, and above all, the action that takes place on the altar—all this is addressed to God. In comparison, Protestant worship is subjective; subjective at times to the point of being anthropocentric. So much of what transpires is addressed to man rather than to God. Or would it be in the interest of accuracy to say that God is addressed in order to speak to man? Prayers are sometimes sermons in disguise! Though it behooves one to speak guardedly here, it can be said that when worship is predominantly objective, as it is in the mass, the I-Thou relationship tends to be formal rather than personal, remote rather than intimate.

The mass is complete in itself, independent of the competence and the character of the celebrant; likewise independent of the laity or the congregation. The mass may be performed and is performed whether worshipers are present or not. It is strictly an oblation offered *ad majorem gloriam dei*. The attendance or participation of people is incidental. If the advocates of liturgical reform within Catholicism are correct in claiming that a substantial proportion of worshipers do not understand what is going on in the mass, then lay participation must indeed be minimal. That something is amiss is supported by the insistent and persistent demand to have the mass celebrated in the vernacular. Whatever may be said for objective worship—and there is much to be said in its favor—this kind of objectivity that plays down personal involvement falls short of the biblical understanding of worship.

Protestant worship, on the other hand, is often highly subjective. The edification of the worshiper is considered to be the major concern. In the words of Willard Learoyd Sperry, "the test of the service is to be its intelligibility and its practicality. The plain man must be able to understand all that takes place, and what takes place must concern his life. Mystery yields place to sound common sense, and wonder is superseded by edification."[16] Protestant Christianity, it must be admitted, has tended to regard worship not so much in terms of the glorification of God as the edification and sanctification of man. If the worshiper has had his emotions aroused, if he has had a religious experience, if he can point to a feeling fond though fugitive, he is presumed to have worshiped.

In reality he may have been engaged in nothing other than some form of self-analysis, self-hypnotism, or self-improvement. The whole peace-of-mind cult, now happily not as vocal as it was formerly, is unadulterated subjectivism. It is not communion with God but with oneself; it is playing with one's feelings. The not uncommon query "Have you tried religion?" or when virtually everything else has failed the suggestion "Why not try religion?" reduces the worship of God, if not God himself, to a utility. Subjectivism in one form or another has colored, and sometimes corrupted, Protestant worship far too much and all too long.

It can be said to the credit of Protestant Christianity that considerable progress has been made in checking, if not eliminating, some of the most blatant aspects of subjectivism. Subjective hymns, for instance, no longer dominate congregational singing as they did in the early decades of this century; sentimental anthems are on the wane; and kerygmatic preaching, though still far too rare, is replacing the shallow, hortatory, topical, sensational variety.

However, Protestant Christianity is not yet out of the woods in this respect. And prospects for a complete recovery from the infection of subjectivism are none too bright. The source of infection, once laid at the doorstep of pietism and a theology of feeling attributed to Schleiermacher, is now to be found in the current preoccupation with the psychology of religion and the philosophy of religion, and also with the sociology of the church in suburbia and the inner city. The liturgical renaissance does not appear to be of much help at this point, especially where theological uncertainty is in the air.

A liturgy may reduce subjective elements to a minimum, but what if there is no objective reality to which man can relate himself? If liturgy could provide the answer to theological uncertainty, Bishop Robinson of *Honest to God* fame should not be as perplexed as his book leads one to believe him to be, for he stands in a liturgical tradition that can hardly be accused of being unduly subjective.[17] It may well be that a good many avant-garde intellectuals are caught up in a new form of theological subjectivism that replaces the God "who is above all and through all and in all" (Eph. 4:6) with something that is a substitute for deity. The remedy for this predicament is not more liturgy but faith in the God who "spoke of old to our fathers by the prophets; but in these last days . . . has spoken to us by a son" (Heb. 1:1-2).

All this underscores once more the importance of theology for liturgical renewal. When the church is either unable or unwilling to make any forthright affirmations about God, it is futile to take refuge in liturgy. The spiritual malaise brought on by secularism, existentialism, and the demythologizing of scripture calls first of all for a theological renewal. While this observation extends beyond the scope of the study at hand, it is nonetheless germane to the discussion, for it points up the importance of the I-Thou relationship in worship.

From worship as encounter with God, it is but a short step to worship as renewal. Renewal is the fruit of worship. This can be said without in any way reducing worship to a utility. What happens *when* man worships is not to be confused with *why* he worships. This is an important distinction to remember. To worship with the end in view of deriving some special benefit, however lofty that benefit may be, may well be something less than pure worship. As previously pointed out, God is to be worshiped because he is God, and not because of anything one may get from him by way of reward. It should be noted also that one of the reasons worship yields so little by way of transforming life is because the quest for benefits obstructs the vision of God. All too often worshipers do not allow themselves to be addressed by God because of the multitude of blessings they ask of God.

When worship is a genuine divine-human encounter, it produces personal renewal. The testimony of the Bible is clear about this. Though in the main it tells us that God is to be worshiped because he is the Lord of life and history, it also assures us that "he rewards those who seek him" (Heb. 11:6).

It has already been mentioned that something happened to the prophet Isaiah when he was confronted by the majesty of God in the temple during the year that King Uzziah died. His sin was forgiven; he received and accepted a commission to serve. Of the many similar episodes recorded in the Scriptures at least two are pertinent to this discussion. The first is Jacob's strange dream at Bethel on his first night away from home. In his dream he saw a ladder extending from heaven to earth with the angels of God ascending and descending. This is first a symbol of the I-Thou relationship that comes into its own when man really worships. But the aftermath is equally important. This encounter marked the beginning of Jacob's moral and spiritual renewal. It is true that another midnight encounter of a similar nature many years later was necessary before Jacob became Israel, the man who had striven with God and had seen him face to face. Without experiencing these two encounters and the transformation that ensued from them, Jacob would hardly have been worthy of standing in the patriarchal tradition.

The other biblical episode that has a bearing on this matter of renewal occurred on the Mount of Transfiguration. Peter, James, and John were not engaged in any formal act of worship, but there can be no doubt that the splendor of the heavenly vision moved them to worship. Without benefit of either an invitation or a liturgy, they worshiped as they probably had never worshiped before. "They fell on their faces, and were filled with awe" (Matt. 17:6). This was such a stimulating experience that Peter wanted to bask in its glow permanently. "If you wish," he said, "I will make three booths here, one for you and one for

Moses and one for Elijah" (Matt. 17:4). Peter, who on several other occasions was very much concerned about himself, was so moved that he became completely oblivious of his personal comfort. Worship is a cleansing, vitalizing, sanctifying act because when man is completely emptied of all self-concern, God enters in and takes over with the result that the course of life is set in the direction of holiness and service.

Perhaps the beneficent effect of worship is most beautifully summed up in the words of the aged Simeon after he had witnessed the presentation of the Christchild in the temple: "Lord, now lettest thou thy servant depart in peace, according to thy word; for mine eyes have seen thy salvation which thou hast prepared in the presence of all peoples" (Luke 2:29-31).

iii · BIBLICAL AND THEOLOGICAL
   PRESUPPOSITIONS

Man's worship is determined by his understanding of God. If God is conceived as a celestial potentate, his devotees will employ elaborate ceremonial rites to flatter his vanity; if God is considered as being remote and indifferent, long and loud incantations, perhaps even self-mutilations will be resorted to in order to arouse his attention and pity (1 Kings 18:28); if he is thought of as an angry and aggrieved deity, he must be placated and propitiated with animal or even human sacrifices to cause him to relent. The religions of mankind make it clear that cultic patterns and practices are shaped by a people's conception of the deity they worship. Theology does indeed shape the liturgy. The first question to be asked of any liturgy is: What are its theological presuppositions? Concerning the liturgy of the church the question is: What is the Christian conception of God?

The answer to this question is not found in science or philosophy, not even in the church's tradition, but in the Bible. In keeping with Luther's appeal to Holy Writ as the final authority, it is good Protestant procedure to search the Scriptures. Obviously the Christian conception of God is not spelled out in the form of carefully worded propositions, for the biblical writers were not and did not presume to be systematic theologians. Nor were they metaphysicians who speculated about the nature of God in the manner of the Greek philosophers. Conceptual thinking was foreign to Hebrew mentality. The Hebrews had no inclination to determine the nature of God per se. As a matter of fact, the secrecy of the Godhead was deemed to be inviolable. The Deuteronomist declared: "The secret things belong to the Lord our God; but the things that are revealed belong to us and to our children forever" (Deut. 29:29). Any attempt to define God was considered impertinent to the point of being impious and insolent. According to the author of Exodus, even Moses was not permitted to see God's *face*. As the divine glory passed by, he had to stand in the cleft of the rock, and then only did he behold God's *back* (Exod. 33:22–23).

Yet there was no uncertainty in Israel regarding the nature of God. Figuratively speaking, a Jacob or an Isaiah might say, "I have seen God face to face" (Gen. 32:30), or "My eyes have seen the King, the Lord of hosts" (Isa. 6:5); but seeing God really meant seeing what he was doing or had done. The Hebrew poets, prophets, and historians drew their conclusions regarding the nature of God from their observations of his action in nature and history; and in a similar way, so did the New Testament writers. In Jesus Christ, God had acted decisively; in him the Word had become flesh; in his face men had beheld the glory of the Father full of grace and truth. It was no empty boast, therefore, when the apostle Paul declared on Mars Hill that he would proclaim the unknown God to whom the Athenians had erected an altar.

Christian worship is and always must be predicated on the

understanding of God as it is unfolded in the Scriptures, and above all in the person of Jesus Christ. For the Christian community, Jesus Christ is God's supreme act of self-disclosure. In turning to the Bible we find four concepts of God that must be regarded as definitive for the ordering of Christian worship. These are God's universality, which means that he is limited neither by race nor space; God's holiness, which includes both the numinous and the ethical; God's righteousness, which defines his dealings with mankind; and God's mercy, which overarches every divine attribute and action.

God's Universality

A long struggle lies behind the concept of divine universality, on which worship in the Judeo-Christian tradition is predicated. Two distinct stages should be noted. The first was the struggle to bring about an acknowledgment that the God of the patriarchs, and he alone, is the God of Israel. This belief that had been acknowledged in principle ever since the time of God's covenant with Abraham and was later written into law at Mount Sinai was repeatedly denied in practice at the altars of Baal and various other deities native to Palestine. The prophets Elijah and Elisha bore the brunt of this struggle and were in no small measure responsible for bringing it to a successful conclusion. The price of victory, however, may have been almost too great. For by claiming exclusive allegiance for Yahweh, worship was restricted to two places—to Bethel in the Northern kingdom and Jerusalem in the Southern kingdom—so that in the process God became severely localized.

Regarding the main stream of Judaism, the temple, more specifically the holy of holies within the temple where the ark of the covenant rested, was considered the dwelling place of the Most High. So completely was the presence of God identified with the temple that the exiles in Babylon wept because, as they said, they could not "sing the Lord's song in a foreign land" (Ps. 137:4). This was more than ordinary homesickness. What troubled them was how they could properly worship Yahweh in Babylon when his dwelling place was in Jerusalem. Another evidence of this identification of God with the temple was the fact that the temple was considered an impregnable fortress. Here the Jews sought refuge as late as A.D. 72 when the Roman army invaded Jerusalem and demolished the city.

It is probable, however, that the Babylonian captivity did affect Hebrew thought by undercutting the severe localization of God. The exiles made the best of a trying situation, and in the process discovered that God could be worshiped away from the temple. Sometime later, exactly when and where is unknown, the synagogue came into being. Although the Jerusalem temple continued to be the special abode of God, synagogue worship proved to be a reasonably satisfactory substitute for temple worship. Therefore, with the introduction of worship in the synagogue, God's presence was simultaneously decentralized and delocalized.

The other phase of the struggle to establish God's universality had racial rather than spatial implications. Its outcome had less bearing on worship than on the spread of the gospel in the Gentile world. From Amos to the end of the Old Testament era, the prophets themselves were concerned with this issue. No such dramatic incident as Elijah's contest with the priests of Baal on Mount Carmel marks its history, but the controversy was every bit as great. That Israel's God was also the God of Israel's foes met with stubborn resistance. The Jews were reluctant to let go of what they were sure was their preferred position. Deutero-Isaiah and Jonah, along with Amos and Jeremiah, deserve special recognition for bringing about the acknowledgment of God's universal sovereignty. Even so, pockets of provincial theism persisted as late as the time of John the Baptist, who, it will be recalled, reminded his countrymen that "God is able from these stones to raise up children to Abraham" (Luke 3:8).

Important as the successful outcome of this particular struggle was in spreading Christianity, the earlier endeavor had a more direct bearing on worship because all through history in the pre-Christian era, in both paganism and Judaism, every deity was closely identified with a sanctuary or sacred place. To this day the place of worship is commonly spoken of as the house of God. Services of worship are frequently begun with the declaration: "The Lord is in his holy temple; let all the earth keep silence before him" (Hab. 2:20). Up to a point this is true. But the place of worship is more appropriately designated as the *house of the church*. A sanctuary is God's house only insofar as he is with his people when they assemble there. "For where two or three are gathered in my name, there am I in the midst of them" (Matt. 18:20)—this is the way Jesus put it. The emphasis is on people and their purpose for assembling, not on place.

A faint recognition of this truth can be traced back to the time of Solomon, or, if not to him, then to the later historian recording the events of Solomon's reign. In the prayer dedicating the temple, Solomon said: "But will God indeed dwell on the earth? Behold, heaven and the highest heaven cannot contain thee; how much less this house which I have built" (1 Kings 8:27). If Solomon or his historian entertained some doubt at this point, Deutero-Isaiah did not. Without any reservation he declared: "For thus says the high and lofty One who inhabits eternity, whose name is Holy: 'I dwell in the high and holy place, and also with him who is of a contrite and humble spirit'" (Isa. 57:15). For him the locale was not a matter of great importance.

Psalm 139 incorporates beyond doubt the most comprehensive acknowledgment of God's universality to be found in the Old Testament. According to the author of this poem there is no place in the highest heaven or the deepest hell, in the thickest darkness or the brightest light, where God is not present. He is not confined to some distant realm "up there" or "out there"; on the contrary, he knew God to be "closer than breathing and nearer than hands and feet,"[1] for God had discerned his innermost thoughts. God is declared to be acquainted with all his ways. His eyes beheld the poet's unformed substance before he was born. And the poet rejoiced that it was so. Here God is conceived to be entirely free and independent of any and every special locale.

Not to be overlooked in this connection is the conversation of Jesus with the woman of Samaria. She wanted to know whether one must worship in Jerusalem, as the Jews claimed, or "on this mountain"—presumably near Jacob's well—where her people worshiped. Jesus replied: "The hour is coming, and now is, when the true worshipers will worship the Father in spirit and truth, for such the Father seeks to worship him. God is spirit, and those who worship him must worship in spirit and truth" (John 4:23-24). This word definitely undercuts any attempt to localize God in a given place. The apostle Paul underscored it when he said to the Athenians: "The God who made the world and everything in it, being Lord of heaven and earth, does not live in shrines made by man, nor is he served by human hands, as though he needed anything, since he himself gives to all men life and breath and everything" (Acts 17:24-25).

GOD'S HOLINESS

Of the various attributes ascribed to God, holiness is doubtless one of the oldest. In today's use of the term, holiness has connotations of purity and perfection. In early Hebrew history it was not, however, so much linked with what was moral or ethical as with what was mysterious and mystifying. According to Millar Burrows holiness meant "the numinous quality of Deity, the *mysterium tremendum,* or, more particularly, the 'otherness' of God, his separation from everything ordinary, earthly, or human."[2] So God is spoken of as dwelling "in thick darkness" (1 Kings 8:12) or, as Paul put it, "in unapproachable light" (1 Tim. 6:16). Both phrases suggest that what God is in his very being cannot be fully known. The divine otherness incites awe and wonder; the Old Testament words most frequently used to describe man's response are "fear and trembling."

This emphasis on fear and trembling is particularly pronounced in the so-called Enthronement Psalms (47, 93, 95-100), which are presumed to have been sung as an accompaniment to a ceremonial procession celebrating Yahweh's sovereignty. Thus Psalm 99 begins with the words: "The Lord reigns; let the peoples tremble! He sits enthroned upon the cherubim; let the earth quake!" Appropriately enough, the poet adds in Ps. 99:5 the further admonition: "Extol the Lord our God; worship at his footstool! Holy is he!" God's holiness simultaneously mystifies and fascinates; it might be said to fascinate because it mystifies.

Holiness, in this sense, is rooted partly in the fact that the divine otherness transcends man's capacity to comprehend the fullness of God's being. But only in part. As far as the Old Testament is concerned, his transcendent power becomes even more impressive by his acts in nature and history. God's overpowering majesty, for instance, is seen in the grandeur of the heavens. "The heavens are telling the glory of God; and the firmament proclaims his handiwork. Day to day pours forth speech, and night to night declares knowledge" (Ps. 19:1-2). Such violent forces of nature as lightning, thunder, whirlwinds, and earthquakes are equally impressive. For when "the voice of the Lord flashes forth flames of fire . . . makes the oaks to whirl, and strips the forests bare" (Ps. 29:7, 9), men are moved to say, "Glory!" Noteworthy too, is the fact that awe-inspiring, if not terrifying, phenomena attended Moses' ascent to the top of Mount Sinai. The mountain "was wrapped in smoke, because the Lord descended upon it in fire . . . and the whole mountain quaked greatly" (Exod. 19:18).

The Hebrews likewise saw manifestations of God's might and majesty in the events of history. Israel's deliverance from bondage in Egypt followed by the conquest of the promised land was a case in point. Not for a moment were the people permitted to forget what Yahweh had done. A lament written many centuries later began with the words: "We have heard with our ears, O God, our fathers have told us, what deeds thou didst perform in their days, in the days of old: thou with thine own hand didst drive out the nations. . . . Not by their own sword did they win the land, nor did their own arm give them victory; but thy right hand, and thy arm, and the light of thy countenance; for thou didst delight in them" (Ps. 44:1-3). The spectacular defeat of the priests of Baal on Mount Carmel was still another manifestation of God's might and majesty.

Dramatic events of this nature, and some less dramatic, helped to create the image of God's holiness. Consequently it behooved man to "worship the Lord in holy array" (1 Chron. 16:29). The sentiment expressed in Psalm 8 is fairly typical of the Hebrew mind as it reflected on the majesty of God. Although man's kinship with God is acknowledged, the overall emphasis is focused on God's incomprehensible infinity: "What is man that thou art mindful of him, and the son of man that thou dost care for him?" (Ps. 8:4).

Gradually, however, the concept of holiness underwent a marked change. In both the priestly and the prophetic traditions, holiness took on the quality of the ethical, not so much supplanting the numinous as supplementing it. The key word of the Holiness Code found in Leviticus 19-26 is "You shall be holy; for I the Lord your God am holy" (Lev. 19:2). However, the priestly understanding of holiness and the prophetic understanding of it move out from this common center in two different directions.

In the priestly tradition, the appropriate response to the holiness of God was conceived of primarily in cultic terms. Faithfulness in meeting the requirements of the cult had priority over moral uprightness. The temple and the temple cult became holy in themselves, for they were set apart, or sanctified, to serve a holy Lord. One is tempted to say that something akin to an *ex opere operato* holiness came to be equated with the temple cult. The meticulous regulations, covering everything from the proper ceremonial garb of the officiating priests to the proper preparation of the animals to be sacrificed, point in this direction. It was assumed that thank offerings and trespass offerings expressed the attitude of the worshiper, yet the cultic act had an efficacy by itself. As J. Coert Rylaarsdam points out, "There was no virtue in the blood of the sacrifices of the Day of Atonement, apart from liturgical actions in which it functioned." He continues by saying, "A repentant spirit, however important and however genuine, was no substitute for the actual ceremony of Atonement. According to the Mishnah repentance was essential if one were to participate in the fruits of the Day of Atonement; on the other hand, not the repentance but the holy day and its ordinances effect atonement."[3]

From the prophetic perspective the temple cult compromised the holiness of God, at least in practice if not in principle. Amos, Isaiah, Hosea, and Micah inveighed against the cult, not on grounds of ceremonial casualness or laxness, but on grounds of ethical irrelevance. Ceremonially speaking, what the priesthood did was above reproach; if anything, the priests were overzealous and meticulous in preparing the offerings and oblations in accordance with every detail prescribed by the Levitical code. The issue that the prophets raised was whether divine holiness needed such a lavish cult; whether, in fact, it had anything to do with holiness at all. God's holiness, they declared, is first and foremost ethical in character.

Divine holiness so conceived calls for nothing less than obedience. In Micah 6:8, the prophet asks, "What does the Lord require of you but to do justice, and to love kindness, and to walk humbly with your God?" Isaiah was equally explicit. "Wash yourselves; make yourselves clean; remove the evil of your doings from before my eyes; cease to do evil, learn to do good; seek justice, correct oppression; defend the fatherless, plead for the widow" (Isa. 1:16-17). Whether Isaiah and Micah along with Amos and Hosea were ready to throw the temple cult out bag and baggage is debatable; but there is no question that they had a different understanding of God's holiness and what it required of man than the one on which the temple cult was predicated. From their perspective ceremonial correctness did not meet the requirements of divine holiness.

For obvious reasons the prophetic emphasis was seldom very popular. The advantages were all on the side of priestly religion. It was enshrined in a cult hallowed by a practice going back to the days of Moses and Aaron; it was domiciled in the temple and watched over by an entrenched and disciplined priesthood. Priestly religion also had great appeal to the senses. People could see and smell the burnt offerings as they were consumed by fire on the altar. In comparison, prophetic religion was too exacting in its ethical demands, too austere in its simplicity. There was no cult or institution to perpetuate it. For its preservation the prophetic emphasis was dependent on an occasional voice crying in the wilderness. And that voice had no other credentials than a "Thus saith the Lord."

Nevertheless, the prophetic emphasis, so often carried by a dissenting voice, was destined to sway the future. There is no question as to which of the two strands of Judaism—the priestly or the prophetic—has had the most lasting influence. Even though prophetic religion lost much of its pristine purity in the legalism of the scribes and Pharisees—whom Jesus accused of tithing mint, dill, and cummin while leaving undone the weightier matters of justice and mercy—it nevertheless molded both Judaism and Christianity.

Jesus stood squarely within the prophetic tradition. Like the prophets before him, he conceived of holiness primarily in ethical terms. His precepts and parables make that abundantly clear. He warned against making a show of piety; heaping up empty phrases in prayer, he declared, was pagan and fasting for the sake of fasting was meaningless. If by chance a man should come to worship while estranged from his brother, he would first need a reconciliation with his brother before God would consider his offering acceptable. A priest and Levite on their way to the temple stood condemned because they passed a wounded traveler on the way without stopping to render assistance. Access to the kingdom will not be given to anyone for saying "Lord, Lord" while failing to do the will of the Father in heaven. These and many other teachings place the emphasis unmistakably on the ethical.

There is no word on record of Jesus with regard to his support of the temple cult. The way it was abused angered him to the point of driving out all the merchants and money changers who had converted the Father's house of prayer into a marketplace. His denunciation of the scribes and Pharisees, charging them with being full of hypocrisy and iniquity while outwardly appearing to be righteous, lend support to the judgment that legalism, along with ceremonialism, fails to conform to the holiness of God.

Worship must take into account both aspects of divine holiness. Hebrew worship did so, particularly in the postexilic period. The psalter, generally recognized to have been the hymnbook of the second temple, bears witness on this score. In psalm after psalm God's unfathomable majesty is extolled. Though man has been made a "little less than God" (Ps. 8:5), as a psalmist declared, this "little less" is considerable. Man may have dominion over the works of God's hands, but it is a God-given dominion. In comparison, modern man is constantly tempted to claim all the credit for his remarkable mastery over nature. Today's generation does not easily feel the awe and wonder that caused a Hebrew poet to exclaim, "How precious to me are thy thoughts, O God! How vast is the sum of them!" (Ps. 139:17). We are too impressed with our own scientific and technological achievements to recognize the infinitely greater wisdom and power of the Creator.

The moral earnestness that runs through the psalter does not come easily to us. A familiar hymn begins with the phrase, "Just as I am, without one plea"; modern man is more inclined to say, "Just as I am, without one apology." Man's sense of mastery over nature carries over into the moral realm. He considers himself to be as competent morally as he is technologically. Such concessions and accommodations that are made to the mores of society are not generally considered to be very serious. Consequently the psalmist's admonition to worship God in holy array is more apt to be associated with the holiness of beauty than the beauty of holiness. But God's holiness requires clean hands and a pure heart. It calls for humility and obedience, for justice and mercy in all areas of life.

THE RIGHTEOUSNESS OF GOD

The third biblical concept that underlies faith and worship in the Judeo-Christian tradition is the righteousness of God. As a matter of fact, it figures more prominently in the biblical understanding of God than the concept of holiness. More is said about God's being righteous than God's being holy. A hurried look at a concordance substantiates this beyond a shadow of

doubt. His righteousness is understood in scripture to be un-
varied and unwavering in its consistency and constancy.

When we speak of righteousness we envisage a person of integrity, one who is honest and upright in conduct. The description given of Job is fairly typical. Of him it is recorded that he
"was blameless and upright, one who feared God, and turned
away from evil" (Job 1:1). In comparison God's righteousness
is much broader; it includes more than uprightness. It defines
God's deeds and relationships rather than describing a quality
of being. By way of sharpening the biblical understanding of
God's righteousness, John Wick Bowman makes the helpful distinction between what is known about "God-in-history" and
"God-in-himself." This is to say, the concept of righteousness is
derived from God's dealings with mankind. God's self-disclosure
in history is by all odds more definitive for faith and worship
than his self-disclosure in nature; but the latter is by no means
insignificant. Professor Rylaarsdam is quite right in reminding us
"that Christianity has perhaps never done full justice to the
role of nature, Protestant worship least of all."[4] What is of interest at this point is the fact that righteousness characterizes all
of God's dealings and relationships with the world.

One facet of this righteousness is trustworthiness. God is reliable. He is consistent in everything he does, never capricious or
arbitrary. He is from everlasting to everlasting the same. He
does not pursue one line today and another tomorrow. Man can
count on him to carry out his threats as well as keep his promises.
"The Lord has sworn," declared a psalmist, "and will not
change his mind" (Ps. 110:4). Again and again the Israelites
drew strength and comfort from the assurance that the promises
of God are yea and amen. When persecution and adversity were
Israel's lot, the poets and prophets kept saying that God could
be counted on to redeem his people. He had done so in the past;
he would do so in the future. The prophecies of Deutero-Isaiah

were filled with assurances that deliverance would come to the exiles. His authority for saying so? "The mouth of the Lord has spoken" (Isa. 40:5).

Judgment is another facet of righteousness. The Lord who sits enthroned "judges the world with righteousness, he judges the people with equity" (Ps. 9:8). This means vindication for the persecuted and oppressed, and punishment for evildoers. Even God's own people are not exempt from his righteous judgments. Amos stated this clearly. He declared, "Thus says the Lord: For three transgressions of Judah, and for four, I will not revoke the punishment; because they have rejected the law of the Lord, and have not kept his statutes" (Amos 2:4).

Righteousness, then, includes both retribution and redemption; it includes his saving grace as well as the dark line in the divine face that will not countenance iniquity. Man can always depend on him to act without pique or partiality, for the "Lord is just in all his ways and kind in all his doings" (Ps. 145:17). To be noted in particular is the adjective all. There is no dichotomy in the sense that God exercises justice in one moment and extends mercy at another. "All that God is is present in all his actions," is the way John Wick Bowman expresses it.[5]

It is not without significance that after Isaiah had spelled out Yahweh's indictment of the temple cult, he followed it with the invitation: "Come now, let us reason together, says the Lord: though your sins are like scarlet, they shall be white as snow; though they are red like crimson, they shall become like wool" (Isa. 1:18). What the prophet meant is that the righteous God of Israel can be worshiped without benefit of animal sacrifices and solemn assemblies. The Lord does not need to be appeased or placated; he is not unreasonable. He is willing to forgive all who come with a humble and contrite heart, and resolve to walk in his ways.

The New Testament underscores this faith in the righteousness of God. In his teachings Jesus did not elaborate on this at any great length. It was hardly necessary for him to emphasize something that had come to be generally accepted. Faith in the righteousness of God undergirded his life from beginning to end. When he stood on the threshold of his ministry, he resolved the issues that confronted him by declaring complete trust and confidence in the revealed will of God (Matt. 4:1-11). This same trust sustained him in his greatest hour of trial in the garden of Gethsemane. His ability to say "Not my will, but thine, be done" (Luke 22:42) was predicated on the conviction that God can be trusted to the uttermost. Confidence in God's righteousness informed his teachings, motivated his decisions, and supported him in his dying hour, even as it has informed all faith and worship in the Judeo-Christian tradition.

It should be stated that as long as the church considered its major responsibility to be that of preparing people for death rather than for the living of these days, judgment was the dominant note in man's conception of God's righteousness. Both Pietism and revivalism stressed retribution. In sermon and song, people were constantly reminded that it was a fearful thing for sinners to fall into the hands of a righteous God. Now that the pendulum has swung from an otherworldly to a this-worldly religion, the righteousness of God may tend to be equated with a kind of grandfatherly indulgence that makes no sharp distinction between good and evil. Insofar as this is true, it is imperative that the cultus of the church be informed anew with the prophetic conception of righteousness which keeps retribution and redemption in tension and in balance.

THE MERCY OF GOD

By way of rounding out the biblical conception of God, a word needs to be said about God's being merciful. He is declared to be merciful and gracious, slow to anger and abounding in steadfast love. Taken from Psalm 103:8, this concept provides some evidence that mercy is by no means exclusively a New Testament concept. It may not have received as much emphasis in the writings of the Hebrew poets and prophets as it does in the New Testament, but the basic conviction is there.

Hosea was the first of the prophets to stress the mercy of God. Speaking for Yahweh he said: "I will betroth you to me for ever; I will betroth you to me in righteousness and in justice, in steadfast love, and in mercy" (Hos. 2:19). A little farther on we read: "My heart recoils within me, my compassion grows warm and tender" (Hos. 11:8). Nor is Hosea the only one to speak of God's being full of mercy and compassion. Isaiah adds his testimony when he writes: "Thou, O Lord, art our Father, our Redeemer from of old is thy name" (Isa. 63:16). Jeremiah is dismayed at Israel's unfaithfulness because of God's known concern for his people. "I thought you would call me, My Father, and would not turn from following me" (Jer. 3:19). The recognition that God is gracious underlies what is doubtless the greatest penitential poem of all time. Only one who knew God to be merciful could possibly have prayed: "Have mercy on me, O God, according to thy steadfast love; according to thy abundant mercy blot out my transgressions" (Ps. 51:1).

The term *steadfast love* occurs too frequently in the Old Testament to escape attention. These two words (*loving-kindness* in the American Standard Version) along with compassion, mercy, goodness, and grace are used again and again. The father image is also pressed into service repeatedly to describe God's relationship to his people. To the passages already quoted from Isaiah and Jeremiah one might add Psalm 103:13: "As a father pities his children, so the Lord pities them who fear him." It seems clear then that a concept of God that stresses his graciousness, mercy, and steadfast love is not uniquely a New Testament concept.

There is far more similarity between the faith of Jesus and his Hebrew forebears than scholars at one time were ready to acknowledge. Jesus placed major emphasis on the divine attribute of steadfast love above all others. The father image controlled his life and dominated his teaching. What he said about God as the heavenly Father who knows the needs of his children even before they ask and who is willing to forgive the wayward and the willful, even to the point of pursuing the lost, is so well-known that documentation is superfluous. To call attention to such parables as the lost coin, the lost sheep, the lost sons, the importunate widow, and the unrighteous steward is all the evidence that is needed. Jesus made it clear that God's fatherly concern and compassion far exceed that of any earthly father. "If you then, who are evil, know how to give good gifts to your children, how much more will your Father who is in heaven give good gifts to those who ask him" (Matt. 7:11).

These four concepts are important to the cultus of the church. First, God is present everywhere at all times and can be worshiped anywhere—under the open sky as well as in a cloistered sanctuary. What is important is not the locale, but that worship be in spirit and truth. Second, God is holy. He is holy in the numinous sense of being transcendent and is holy in the ethical sense of being perfect in his purity. Third, God is righteous in all his doings and relationships; he pursues his purposes with an unwavering constancy in regard to retribution and redemption. Fourth, God is gracious and merciful. Because of his steadfast love, man can come to him with the confidence of a child approaching his father or mother. These are the concepts on which the worship of the church is predicated. If this is the faith that the church professes, it follows that the liturgical forms and practices of the church must be so shaped to embody and reflect this faith.

iv · SANCTUARY AND ALTAR

It may be helpful to reiterate here the basic premise of this study; namely, that liturgical forms and practices must be in harmony with the faith they are intended to express and nurture. This prompts the age-old question of Micah: "With what shall I come before the Lord, and bow myself down before God on high?" The answer must be: Whatever man does or brings when he worships must be in keeping with the character of God. Whether the four divine attributes previously discussed embrace everything that is commonly believed about God in Christendom allows for differences of opinion, but that these four are definitive for the cultus of the church is not subject to debate. Whatever else one may add by way of defining the nature of God, is in one way or another derived from or ancillary to his universality, his holiness, his righteousness, his mercy. In the main these are the touchstones by which the validity or propriety of any cultus form or practice is determined. In all matters of worship, theological principles have priority over any and all liturgical traditions, however much the latter may carry the sanction of antiquity or common usage.

In and by themselves liturgical traditions do not offer authentic guidelines in determining the worship practices of the church. It is a well-known fact that in the course of time a cultus tends to become overlaid with embellishments that either obscure or contradict the faith of the church. Hence, it is extremely important that every liturgical form or practice be evaluated, not so much in the light of its history, but in the light of what the church believes.

Historically speaking, Friedrich Heiler may be right when he declares that "the ultimate basis of all Christian liturgy is . . . the public worship of the primitive Christian community."[1] But this immediately raises the question: Is it possible to reconstruct the pattern of early Christian worship? The answer is: only in a general way. Although the New Testament contains references to the cultic life of the early church, it does not present anything resembling an order of worship. Inferences can be drawn from the Epistles, and to a lesser extent from the four Gospels, notably the fourth.

Liturgiologists who have made a careful study of both the New Testament sources and the cultus of the church in the first century are reasonably certain that the Liturgy of the Word, as distinguished from the Liturgy of the Upper Room, was largely patterned after synagogue worship. This part of the service, which Dom Gregory Dix speaks of as the *Synaxis*, was "simply a continuation of the Jewish synagogue service of our Lord's time."[2] Basically this had four elements: the reading of the Scriptures, the preaching of the word, prayers, and psalmody. There is a striking similarity between synagogue worship and early Christian worship in both form and content. This is not at all surprising. The God and Father of our Lord Jesus Christ was the God of the patriarchs and prophets. All of the teachings of Jesus

are deeply rooted in the rich lore of Hebrew history and prophecy. Little wonder, then, that the apostles, who were Jews,
should borrow freely from the treasures of the Hebrew cultus with
which they had grown up. And since synagogue worship was
basically free of the sacerdotalism inherent in the temple cult,
it was readily adaptable for Christian worship. Moreover, the
historical, prophetic, and poetic books of the Old Testament
were the only liturgical resources available until the Gospels
and Epistles were written and circulated. In short, the Christian
cultus did not start de novo.

Although this much is known about worship in the apostolic
period, it is hardly of great value in determining the content and
structure of the church's worship. Furthermore, no useful purpose
would be served by attempting to reconstruct and impose a
first-century cultus upon the church of the twentieth century.
The whole social, scientific, economic, and cultural milieu of our
day is so different from that of the Near East nineteen hundred
years ago that what was meaningful then is not necessarily
meaningful today. The secular climate of our time poses enough
theological problems without increasing the present-day dilemma
by introducing worship patterns foreign to our age and understanding. One element alone is constant as far as the cultus of
the church is concerned—its faith in the God who revealed himself by his mighty deeds in nature and history. Any deviation at
this point is tantamount to substituting a philosophical system
or an ethical code for faith in the God and Father of our Lord
Jesus Christ. So much by way of general preface. Now some
questions should be considered that revolve around the place
and purpose of sanctuary and altar.

THE HOUSE OF THE CHURCH

Our Lord's declaration that the time had come when true
worshipers would worship the Father in spirit and truth is a

good principle with which to begin. What Jesus said to the woman of Samaria put the capstone on the prophetic endeavor not only to bring all cultic practices into harmony with morality but also to delocalize them as well. This was fortunate in more ways than one; for as Franklin Young points out in an essay, "the New Testament church had no *holy place,* spatially located, which could be designated as *the place* where God, in some special sense, was present to his people."[3] The lack of a special place was largely circumstantial. Being a persecuted minority, the early Christians had neither the right nor the resources to acquire or erect a house of worship.

It is important to mention that they did not need a *holy* place. At this point, Christian worship had a radically different orientation than worship in either the Jewish or the pagan tradition. In the Christian tradition a sanctuary is not the house of God in the same sense in which the Jews regarded the temple to be the special dwelling of Yahweh. Possibly this may explain why the Jews did not actually worship *in* the temple; they assembled for worship in the court of the temple where the altar stood. Strictly speaking, the building we call a church is a *domus ecclesiae,* the house of the church; not *domus dei,* the house of the Lord. In the New Testament Epistles there are casual references to "the church in your house" (Phil. 2) and the church "in her house" (Col. 4:15). It is not likely that these have any other significance than to identify the place where a given church was accustomed to assemble. But it is significant that in the early centuries of the church's life, the term *domus ecclesiae* seems to have been commonly used to designate the place where Christians assembled for worship.

To speak of a sanctuary as being the house or home of the church is not to say that it is improper to regard it also as the house of the Lord. In effect it becomes the house of the Lord because within its four walls the divine-human encounter takes place, at least more often than anywhere else. But the sanctuary has no holiness *an sich.* "The God who made the world and everything in it," said Paul to the Athenians, "does not live in shrines made by man" (Acts 17:24). Long before it became axiomatic in Christendom to say "Where Christ is, there is the church," believers had lived by this principle. Christ is in the koinonia, not in the building. If anything is certain about worship in the apostolic period it is that it centered around the promise: "For where two or three are gathered in my name, there am I in the midst of them" (Matt. 18:20). While Christ was deemed to be uniquely present in the breaking of bread, his presence was not restricted to the Eucharist. The two Emmaus disciples recognized the risen Lord "when he was at table with them, took the bread and blessed it, and broke it" (Luke 24:30), but it would be reading too much into this text to claim that this was the Lord's Supper.

It is true, of course, that the celebration of the Eucharist was at the same time a celebration of Christ's presence. It should be noted, however, that his presence was not localized *in* the elements *on* the table; his presence was *in* the fellowship gathered *around* or *at* the table. Unfortunately, the distinction between *in* the elements *on* the table, on the one hand, and *at* the table, on the other, became obscured by a cult of sacerdotalism completely foreign to the thought and practice of the apostolic community. A living relationship became subordinated to a substantive presence.

ALTAR AND EASTWARD POSITION

With the liturgical renaissance there has emerged a practice that indirectly or unwittingly tends to localize God by the prominence that is given to the altar. Thus Scott Brenner, an early and ardent advocate of liturgical reform, writes: "Whatever the fabric or form of the Altar, we must ever accord it the place of honor and the position most prominent in the church building, for the Altar is in reality the 'House of God,' or the holy place of God, and all corporate worship rightly centers in and about it."[4] The New Testament contains nothing to support this view. It stems from the Roman mass, which began to take its present shape as early as the third or fourth century. The theological presuppositions of the mass may warrant the preeminence that the altar has in Catholicism. They also provide a reasonable justification for the eastward position (the minister facing the altar for prayer) as over against the basilican position (the minister facing the congregation). However, unless Protestant Christianity is ready to reject the letter to the Hebrews, it cannot recognize the validity of what is presumed to take place in the mass nor the validity of various cultic practices associated with the mass. The Eucharist is not a bloodless reenactment of the sacrifice of Christ on the cross.

The reason generally given for facing the altar for prayer, the creed, and the gloria is that thereby the minister identifies himself with the congregation in addressing God. For its symbolism, if for no other reason, it is said, a distinction should be made between addressing the congregation in the reading of the Scriptures and the preaching of the Word, on the one hand, and addressing God in prayer and confession, on the other hand. If this is a valid distinction, then the eastward position should be taken consistently at every point where God is addressed, whether in prayer and confession, or, for that matter, in the singing of certain hymns. But there is no consistency at this point. In some instances the invocation is offered at the lectern or in the center of the chancel from the basilican position, but for the general or pastoral prayer the minister faces the altar. Some ministers lead the congregation in the confession of faith with back turned to the congregation; others face the congregation. In the latter instance it is not unusual for both clergy and choir to turn to the altar for the gloria with a precision resembling a military salute.

If it is proper to face the altar for the gloria, which is addressed to God, is it not equally proper that the same position be taken when hymns addressed to God are sung? Approximately one half of the hymns in the average hymnal embody the I-Thou relationship; that is, God is spoken to by pastor and people. This being the case, a minister concerned about the proper liturgical position should examine the text of every hymn to be sung to ascertain in advance when he should face the altar and when he should face the congregation. If perchance a given hymn should embody the double motif of speaking *to* God in one stanza and *about* God in another, this might present something of a problem, or call for fancy footwork. Let not this last suggestion be taken too seriously. It is offered only to say that liturgical concerns tend to get out of hand.

An example of liturgical punctiliousness appeared in a seminary bulletin, presumably published by the student body. A brief item pertaining to the use of the Apostles' Creed began with the sentence: "Please watch your verbal punctuation!" The writer went on to say that in order to make the meaning of the third article of the Apostles' Creed clear, it is important to note that the phrases "the Holy Christian Church" and "the Communion of Saints" refer to the same body. Hence, he argued, the pause between these two phrases should be shorter than between the other phrases of the creed. One might raise the question whether the post-Nicene fathers would agree with this interpretation. The point is, however, whether the stopwatch precision is essential to a meaningful use of the Apostles' Creed. And the larger concern is whether preoccupation with liturgical niceties does not detract from rather than add to meaningful worship.

Another question should be raised at this juncture. Could it be possible that the eastward position conveys more to worshipers than it is intended to symbolize? The danger at hand is that the altar becomes a uniquely holy place where God in some sense is localized. Scott Brenner is quite frank in saying just that: "God's omnipresence notwithstanding, the worship of the Jewish and Christian peoples has always been a severely localized and directional worship. Indeed, it is wise for us in our worship somewhat to *depreciate* the concept of God's omnipresence."[5] This point of view stands in sharp contradiction to the more advanced thought in Hebrew prophecy; it is tantamount to a denial of the teaching of Jesus in this matter and represents a reversal of the practice in the apostolic church.

In the interest of historical accuracy it should also be pointed out that Christian worship has never been severely localized and directional, at least not in every branch of the church. It certainly was not so in New Testament times. The early Christians, as far as the facts are known, knew nothing of a liturgical east and very likely cared less, for they knew the risen Lord to be present in their midst as he had promised. If direction played any part in their worship, it would logically have been skyward; for living as they did in the confident expectation of an imminent Parousia, they, like the apocalyptists before them, expected the glorified son of man to descend from the heavenly regions above.

Nor has Christian worship been universally directional throughout the centuries. In the Western church, the eastward position did not come into vogue until approximately the tenth century when the altar, for practical reasons, was placed against the "east wall," making it necessary for the celebrant to turn his back to the congregation while celebrating the mass. With the Reformation the altar again became a holy table, and it was placed sufficiently forward in the chancel to enable the clergy to stand behind it and face the congregation. Martin Bucer, who is generally regarded to be the architect of the Lutheran liturgy, was quite emphatic that this should be the position of the altar and the clergy. Even Luther, though inclined to retain those elements of the mass not specifically forbidden by the Scriptures, favored the basilican position. And as far as Zwingli and Calvin are concerned, there can be no doubt where they stood on this issue.

In Walter Lowrie's book *Action in the Liturgy*, a paragraph interpreting the altar as holy table and commenting on the eastward position is so trenchant that it deserves to be quoted in full.

If the altar of the church were simply a place of sacrifice, like every pagan altar, and like the altar of burnt offering outside the tabernacle and temple of the Hebrews, it would be appropriate enough for the priest to go before the people and therefore to turn his back upon them as he leads them to that dread place to which he alone may venture to draw near, and though it would perhaps be rather queer it would not be altogether unseemly to build it like a shelf against the wall. But such was not the Christian tradition for well over a thousand years— and this for the good and sufficient reason that what we call the altar is first and foremost the Holy Table. If calling it an altar obscures the fact that it is a table, we ought to give up calling it an altar. It is the Holy Table which symbolizes the sacramental unity of the church. Accordingly it is appropriate that the church should gather around this table.[6]

If a case is to be made for an altar it will need to be made on the ground that an altar is the symbol of sacrifice—the sacrifice of a humble and contrite heart, the sacrifice of a dedicated life. Since time immemorial man has erected altars on which to present the firstfruits of field and flock to the deity or deities he has worshiped. This practice is as valid today as it was earlier. Sacrifice is a basic ingredient of Christian discipleship; not the sacrifice of propitiation or expiation, but the sacrifice of thanksgiving and dedication. Whether the tithes and offerings presented on the Lord's day are truly sacrificial might be questioned. Yet placing them on the altar is at least symbolic of what man's offering ought to be: a sacrifice and not a collection. If the altar serves the purpose of making this explicit, well and good. Unfortunately, the altar appears to have gained its prominence for more occult reasons.

It is somewhat ironic that twentieth-century Protestant Christianity should be adopting the Catholic practice of placing the altar against the chancel wall at just the time when advocates of liturgical renewal and reform within Catholicism are insisting that the altar be placed far enough away from the chancel wall to allow the celebrant to take the basilican position and face the congregation. In the Netherlands this movement is said to have gained considerable momentum; in the United States, too, some Catholic churches are built with freestanding altars.

From Symbolism to Idolatry

Many churchmen may feel that there is no point in becoming unduly concerned about the location of the altar, the eastward position, or for that matter about any liturgical practice. After all, are not prayers offered from an eastward position as acceptable to God as those offered from the basilican position? The answer is obviously yes. Yet there is reason to be concerned, for an act of worship, however noble in conception and intention, easily begets an erroneous belief. In this instance the practice of altar-facing leads to an unwarranted identification of God with one place or one object in the sanctuary. To all intents and purposes the altar becomes precisely what Scott Brenner and others claim it to be—the focal point of the divine presence. Biblically and theologically this concept is without foundation, and this concept has the added liability of separating earth and altar. Any cultic act that moves in the direction of localizing God in one specific place accentuates the distinction between the secular and the sacred. Christianity, along with the prophetic strand in Judaism, has always regarded this to be fraught with tragic consequences.

It is possible too that a subtle form of idolatry could unwittingly be introduced into the Christian cultus at this point. That is, the altar might become so much an object of veneration that it supplants the God to whom it is dedicated. The apostle Paul declared that the Gentiles had "exchanged the truth about God for a lie and worshiped and served the creature rather than the Creator" (Rom. 1:25). No specifics are given beyond stating that they "exchanged the glory of the immortal God for images resembling mortal man or birds or animals or reptiles" (Rom. 1:23). That which, for want of a better term, might be called "altarology" could easily become idolatry, for idolatry can be committed in a variety of ways.

By way of illustration one might cite the use of icons in Eastern Orthodox worship. According to Evelyn Underhill "the icon gives to the pious Orthodox a genuine sense of the presence of God."[7] It is affirmed that he can pray before it without any risk of idolatry. Undoubtedly this is true, but when by definition the "icon is a place where Christ is present by his grace,"[8] it is difficult to escape the conclusion that symbol and substance are for the most part one and the same. The great veneration in which icons are held lends added support to this conclusion.

Icons are not a problem in Protestant Christianity, but symbols and symbolic actions sometimes are, even though they have a legitimate place in worship. The word of the Lord is communicated through what is seen as well as by what is heard. Only an out-and-out iconoclast would deny that. Yet it is not to be forgotten that the ethical monotheism stemming from Moses and the prophets and moving in a straight line down to Jesus of Nazareth is severely austere about this. Alongside the commandment "You shall have no other gods before me" stands another: "You shall not make yourself a graven image, or any likeness of anything that is in the heaven above, or that is in the earth beneath" (Exod. 20:4). Graven images are not necessarily carved out of wood or marble, or molded from precious metals. A ritual, a genuflection, a chant solemnly intoned, an altar, a crucifix, a cross or the sign of the cross can be given so much prominence and accorded such reverence that in effect the symbol itself comes to be treated as though it were holy.

Cyril C. Richardson has declared that Protestant Christianity must choose "either to return to the iconoclasm of the prophet, and to say that liturgical art is impossible . . . or else to admit the Catholic principle that these hidden depths (of sacramental objects) can be gateways to the Divine."[9] But must the issue be drawn as sharply as that? Is the alternative that clear-cut? If the so-called sacramental objects are gateways to the Divine and no more, they do not necessarily stand in contradiction to Protestant principles and the prophetic tradition.

Paul Tillich is sometimes quoted in support of a more extensive use of "holy" objects in worship because they "become bearers of transcendent power and meaning"; or, as he put it in another context, they become "laden with divine power."[10] He contends that unless Protestant Christianity puts the sacramental principles back into its cultus it is doomed. In another volume Tillich notes "the dynamic character of the religious becomes veiled if some institutions and personalities are considered religious in themselves." This, he contends, seems "to border on blasphemy." He adds, "The meaning of the ritualistic act, as of the sacraments, is not to have holiness in itself, but to be the symbol of the unconditioned, which alone is holy."[11] These statements may not be an outright contradiction, but the capacity to hold these two principles in tension is not given to every man and woman in the pew.

Of Nadab and Abihu, the sons of Aaron, it is recorded that "each took his censer, and put fire in it, and laid incense on it, and offered unholy fire before the Lord, such as he had not commanded them" (Lev. 10:1). The point at issue was not the unholy fire but that a commandment of the Lord had been contemptuously ignored. Similarly, the point at issue in this discussion is not this or that posture or practice, be it the sign of the cross, the eastward position for prayer, the altar, or anything else. The issue is far more fundamental. It is theological. We must ask: What is the theological justification for a particular liturgical practice? What sort of divine image does it presuppose? And even more important, what sort of divine image does it project?

v · CULTUS AND CONDUCT

Cultus and conduct can be set in such sharp juxtaposition that they appear to be antithetical. Some of the writings of the Old Testament prophets tend to create this impression. For instance, Micah's reply to his question, "With what shall I come before the Lord, and bow myself before God on high?" seems to say that the choice is between burnt offerings of animals on the one hand and deeds of justice and kindness on the other (Mic. 6:6-8). However, this could be reading more into his words than he intended to say. Whether Micah, along with others, wanted to abolish the temple cult is open to debate. What is more probable is that the prophetic denunciations were directed not so much against the temple cult itself as against the perversion of the cult. Ceremonial lavishness had taken the place of godliness and moral integrity.

In an earlier prophetic word, the antithesis is not as sharply drawn. When King Saul returned from his victorious expedition against the Amalekites, he brought with him, contrary to the mandate the prophet Samuel had given him, considerable loot in the form of sheep and oxen, ostensibly for the purpose of presenting them as a thank offering to God. In the account of 1 Samuel 15:22, the prophet confronted him with the question: "Has the Lord so great delight in burnt offerings and sacrifices, as obeying the voice of the Lord?" Obedience, said Samuel, is better than sacrifice. Sacrifice is not ruled out, but obedience comes first. Conceivably a sacrifice of thanksgiving might have been considered acceptable and appropriate if a divine mandate had not been ignored.

If the psalter offers any authentic guidelines regarding Hebrew thought in this matter, it can be said that by and large cult and conduct did not stand in sharp juxtaposition. The psalms on the whole are informed by a profound moral earnestness and a genuine appreciation of the temple cult. Many have a pronounced ethical as well as a liturgical character. For example, the questions raised in Psalm 24:3, "Who shall ascend the hill of the Lord? And who shall stand in his holy place?" presuppose an occasion of public worship. The hill of the Lord refers to Jerusalem and the holy place is the temple. A worshiper may not presume to stand in the holy place unless he has clean hands, a pure heart, and has not lifted up his soul to what is false (Ps. 24:4). Moral integrity is the necessary precondition for participation in the cultus of the community. Psalm 51:17 is equally instructive at this point. There is no doubt in the author's mind that "the sacrifice acceptable to God is a broken spirit." This is the first and foremost requirement. But either he, or a later editor (as many Old Testament scholars contend), was confident that when a man came to the temple with a broken and contrite heart, God would then "delight in right sacrifices." In other words, cultus and conduct might well go together. The act of presenting a sin offering might indeed express the contrition and repentance of the worshiper toward God.

More than that, some kind of cultic rite, simple or elaborate,

s necessary to nurture the faith and maintain the spiritual vitality
of a religious community. By the same token, a liturgy is an essential and indispensable vehicle to express and to foster the spirit
of reverence and devotion. Adoration, gratitude, penitence, obedience, commitment, and other responses to God become articulate
in hymns, prayer, creed, and confession; at the same time they are
kindled by appropriate actions in the liturgy. It is important,
therefore, that the liturgy be so ordered that it will accomplish,
as far as man's designing can do so, its intended purpose.

WORSHIP IN HOLY ARRAY

In the Hebrew-Christian tradition, to worship in holy array
meant a recognition of God's holiness. When the psalmist summoned his people to worship in holy array, he had both the
numinous and ethical facets of divine holiness in mind. For the
moment attention should be given to the numinous. The call to
worship, the solemn declaration "In the name of the Father, and
of the Son, and of the Holy Spirit," and the invocation along
with the processional or opening hymn lend themselves admirably
to convey something of God's otherness. For that matter, every
facet of the liturgy should contribute to man's awareness of being
in the presence of a God of infinite majesty and mercy. This has
special bearing upon how God is addressed and on the kind of
language used in prayer.

The intimate chumminess with the Almighty that used to
characterize Protestant worship in some quarters is unseemly, to
say the least. Referring to God, one may assume that it makes
no difference whether he is addressed by the use of the pronoun
thou or *you.* The conversational *you,* however, seems to convey
a lack of reverence. Conceivably this could be a matter of personal
taste or preference; nevertheless, it is significant that in the
Revised Standard Version of the Bible the use of the archaic

thee, thine, and *thou* has been retained wherever the reference
is to God or Jesus Christ. This may be a relatively minor consid
eration, but what is suggested here is that every phase and face
of the liturgy calls for good taste in form and chaste simplicity in
language.

Extemporaneous or free pastoral prayers are sometimes found
wanting in this respect. A poor choice of words, faulty grammar
or flowery speech may not be an abomination before God, but
such things give offense to many people in the pews. Flamboyant
speech must also be considered anathema.

Apropos of public prayers, Henry Sloane Coffin suggests that
they be "composed of short words, with a sparing use of adjec
tives, and with the strength of the sentences in the nouns and
verbs."[1] By way of example one might cite the well-known prayer
for the church by Archbishop Laud.

> Gracious Father, we humbly beseech thee for thy universal
> church. Fill it with all truth, in all truth with all peace
> Where it is corrupt, purge it, and where it is in error, direct it
> where it is superstitious, rectify it; where anything is amiss, re
> form it; where it is right, strengthen and confirm it; where it is
> in want, furnish it; where it is divided and rent asunder, make
> up the breaches thereof, O thou holy One of Israel; for the
> sake of Jesus Christ our Lord and Savior. Amen.[2]

A prayer should never attract attention to itself. This also
applies to the liturgy. Whenever a liturgy is said to be beautiful,
one has reason to suspect that liturgical form has become an end
in itself. This is somewhat like having faith in faith, rather than
faith in God. One criticism leveled at liturgical reform with some
justice is that embellishments are added seemingly on the prin
ciple that if one response is good, two or three are much better. In
some instances the liturgy begins to suffer from what might be
termed "too-muchness." When this happens ceremony becomes
ceremonialism and falls under the admonition of Jesus: "In

raying do not heap up empty phrases as the Gentiles do" (Matt. 6:7).

A religious community has need of a cultus, but it is important to remember that cultus and conduct, worship and work belong together. In a sense they are two sides of the same shield. It has been said, "Christian worship and the Christian moral life constitute an inseparable, indivisible, and indissoluble unity."[3] On that score the testimony of the New Testament letters, along with the Old Testament prophetic books, is unmistakably clear. Noteworthy in this instance is Paul's word in Romans: "I appeal to you therefore, brethren, by the mercies of God, to present your bodies as a living sacrifice, holy and acceptable to God, which is your spiritual worship" (Rom. 12:1). Two terms—sacrifice and worship—are used, but they are not used in an exclusively cultic sense. The injunction that follows, "Do not be conformed to this world but be transformed by the renewal of your mind," makes it clear that the apostle was speaking of man's total response to God, and not just his response at the time of worship (Rom. 12:2). The reference to "a living sacrifice," in contrast to the sacrificed life of an animal, calls for a life that is dedicated at all times.

In the apostolic church the line dividing cultus and conduct, liturgy and life, worship and work was not drawn as sharply as it was in the centuries that followed. Alexander Schmemann, dean of St. Vladimir's Theological Seminary, contends that "the Christian *leitourgia* is not a 'cult' if by this term we mean a sacred action, or rite, performed in order to establish 'contact' between the community and God."[4] As a matter of fact, very little is mentioned about strictly cultic matters in the New Testament, with the exception of what is told about the Lord's Supper.

The Gospels report the occasion and the words of its institution. On the basis of Paul's reference to the practice in the church at Corinth, we may conclude that the pattern set in the

Upper Room was followed rather faithfully. The apostle point
out—perhaps to disprove the allegation of preaching anothe
gospel—that he had "delivered" what he had "received from th
Lord" (1 Cor. 11:23). He then proceeds to give a very brie
account of what appears to have been standard procedur
throughout the church. This is the nearest thing to a formal o
formulated liturgy to be found in the New Testament.

THE PRIORITY OF THE ETHICAL

What is of immediate interest is the fact that the apostle Pau
appears to have been more concerned about the character an
conduct of the communicants than about the precise manner i
which the Eucharist was to be observed. Special emphasis i
placed on worthy participation. This calls for a reconciliation o
estranged members, for sobriety in eating and drinking at th
agape, and above all for a critical self-examination, lest a ma
eat and drink judgment upon himself. It is clear that receivin
the bread and wine of the Eucharist was not considered to b
meritorious or efficacious by itself. The Eucharist could hav
meaning only when the communicant came to the Lord's tabl
with a contrite heart and faith in the risen Lord and Savio

Paul's first Corinthian letter is particularly instructive at th
point of underscoring the ethical in the total life of that Chris
tian fellowship. The problems within the church, whether of
strictly cultic or a more general communal nature, are deal
with from the perspective of a Christian's high calling. The issu
whether it would be right for Christians to eat meat offered t
idols was resolved by appealing to what would be helpful t
fellow believers rather than by some legal standard of right an
wrong. Preparing a sumptuous meal for the agape preceding th
Eucharist was discouraged because those with little to eat woul
be embarrassed. Pretensions of importance were declared to hav
no place in a Christian fellowship, for the body of Christ—jus

like the human body—has "weaker" and "less honorable" members. If anything, these should be accorded greater honor.

Of special significance in this connection is that exquisite prose poem on love found in 1 Corinthians 13. So complete in itself, it is seldom seen in its relationship to the situation that appears to have provoked it. Its *Sitz im Leben* is the corporate life and cultus of the church. By no means is it to be regarded as a digression from the main line of thought. Although this chapter contains no specific reference to the worship life of the Corinthian church, cultual implications are not hard to detect. What is said by way of downgrading eloquence and erudition in 1 Corinthians 13:1-3 had a direct bearing on glossolalia. Although Paul was ready to concede that ability to speak in tongues might be a special charisma of the Spirit, he nevertheless insisted that this gift must be exercised with due restraint. As for himself, he deemed it better to speak five words that would be understood than ten thousand in a tongue (1 Cor. 14:19). Everything that is said in praise of love and about giving up childish ways, appears to be pointed at the factionalism and jealousies that are spoken of in the first part of the letter.

This letter to the Corinthians is by no means unique in according priority to moral conduct. Though relatively little is said about worship per se, it is important to note that when the cultual practices of the church are mentioned, though for the most part incidentally, the ethical emphasis stands out. When Paul writes, "Let the word of Christ dwell in you richly, as you teach and admonish one another in all wisdom, and as you sing psalms and hymns and spiritual songs with thankfulness in your hearts to God" (Col. 3:16), the reference is obviously to public worship. Teaching and admonition were to have a prominent place in worship. The same emphasis is found in Ephesians 5:18-19: "And do not get drunk with wine, for that is debauchery; but be filled with the Spirit, addressing one another in psalms and hymns and spiritual songs, singing and making melody to the Lord with all your heart." Apparently there were those in Ephesus, just as in the church at Corinth, who imbibed too freely, either before or at the agape. At any rate, the emphasis is on sobriety and wholeheartedness. The latter is the import of making "melody to the Lord with all your heart."

That cultual matters were relatively unimportant can also be deduced from the fact that the liturgy of the primitive church was free and informal. Beyond insisting that "all things should be done decently and in order," the apostle did not lay down any rules regarding the ordering of public worship. Undoubtedly the informality that prevailed in early church worship was a carry-over from synagogue worship, which allowed any worshipers to make contributions if they were so moved. A good example is the occasion when Jesus stood up in the synagogue at Nazareth, read a passage from the book of Isaiah, and then proceeded to interpret it; for it is recorded by Luke that the people "wondered at the gracious words which proceeded out of his mouth" (Luke 4:22).

A similar practice must have prevailed in the early church, since members were encouraged to "teach and admonish" one another, or to address one another in psalms and hymns. The latter suggests that an individual need not necessarily make an original contribution. Quoting a favorite psalm or hymn would be acceptable. Members were also encouraged to speak up in the manner that was customary at testimonial meetings of a former generation. What Paul referred to as "a revelation, a tongue, or an interpretation" (1 Cor. 14:26) may well have been in the nature of a testimonial. To what extent this practice persisted beyond the apostolic period is difficult to surmise—it was probably not for very long! The church's growth in numbers certainly precluded any widespread participation of this nature. Had this become standard practice, the service of worship would surely have become unbearably long. Even in the apostolic period, spontaneous contributions in the form of prophecies and glossolalia got out of hand, perhaps not so much in length as in reverence and orderliness.

When the liturgy became fixed in form and content, all unscheduled and strictly spontaneous contributions from the pew disappeared. At the same time, formal worship ceased to be what the term liturgy, etymologically speaking, implies. It was no longer the work of the people but became more and more the work of the priesthood. In the mass that evolved, something was done for the people rather than by the people. In effect, worshipers became spectators instead of being participants. Advocates of liturgical reform within Catholicism contend that this continues to be the weakness of worship within the Roman Church to this day.

The Reformation sought to correct this situation; first of all, by the use of the vernacular so that people could understand what was being said, and then by the prominence given to hymnody. The importance of hymn singing can hardly be overstated. During the centuries that followed, Protestants have indeed addressed the Lord as well as one another "in psalms and hymns and spiritual songs." Hymn singing, perhaps more than any other part of the liturgy, provides the most complete and satisfying outlet for the people in the pew to contribute something to corporate worship. Today the members of the church do not select the hymns to be sung, as they did at informal song services in the past. In all probability the hymns selected by the minister do not always meet with popular approval but, nevertheless, they do more than put words on the lips of worshipers. One dares to hope that hymns stimulate thought and kindle emotions that would otherwise have remained dormant and inarticulate.

In recent decades, largely because of the liturgical renaissance, the liturgy has been expanded to include choral responses, responsive reading of selected passages of scripture, a period for silent prayer, possibly a prayer litany, or what is known as a bidding prayer. All of these are intended to rescue worship from being a solo performance by the clergy and to make it in fact a corporate act of the people. In the days of revivalism, lay participation was confined largely to interjections such as "Hallelujah," "Amen," and "Praise the Lord." Midweek testimonial services or prayer meetings offered another avenue for lay participation in the worship life of the church. Unfortunately, they had a tendency to become stereotyped; in some instances they were monopolized by a few saints who found delight in making a display of their piety. Rightfully, therefore, they fell into disrepute and slowly died a natural death. All things considered, it is not easy to strike a happy balance between a formal order of worship, which is ever in danger of quenching the Spirit, and a less formal order that gets out of hand and degenerates into uncouth casualness or a wild orgasm of ecstasy.

Cultus and Moral Integrity

The major issue, however, is not one of form or freedom in worship but of preserving the moral integrity of worship. Sincerity and truth are primary requisites. In Christianity as well as in Judaism, man's faith and faithfulness have again and again been measured in terms of cultual regularity rather than in terms of moral uprightness. This is so evident that someone was prompted to make the following cynical observation:

> They're praising God on Sunday,
> They'll be all right on Monday;
> It's just a little habit they've acquired.

In the apostolic and post-apostolic period, the Liturgy of the Word placed the ethical content of Christian faith in the foreground. This became absorbed in the Liturgy of the Upper Room which, however devout in intention, soon became overlaid with ceremonial embellishments reminiscent of the Jewish temple cult and Oriental mystery religions. Just to be present for that climactic moment in the mass when the priest lifted up the transubstantiated elements of bread and wine was deemed to be sufficient. In order to worship, one did not need to attend the mass from beginning to end. In fact, it was not even necessary to receive the elements; witnessing the miracle performed on the altar was enough.

The neglect of the ethical proved to be a double liability and contributed to the perversion of the Eucharist. A whole complex of ideas alien to its origin and purpose became identified with it. Its original character was radically changed. What in apostolic times had been a solemn act of remembrance and joyful anticipation, as well as a means of receiving the freely offered grace of God, became a propitiatory rite performed by the church and presented to God as an offering for sin. A more blatant contradiction of the New Testament faith in the once-for-all sufficiency of Christ's death on the cross is difficult to conceive. Perversions of one kind or another inevitably corrupt worship when the ethical is subordinated to the cultus. Religious ceremonies are ever in danger of degenerating into ceremonialism. Thus, when liturgical renewal ends up in a liturgy that is acclaimed for its *beauty*, ceremonialism, like the camel, has its nose in the tent and, unless restrained, will soon take over the entire cultus.

Perversion of the Christian cultus is not the only liability of ceremonialism. Ceremonialism has the added liability of becoming a substitute for morality—an aspect of the temple cult that alarmed the Old Testament prophets. People brought their offerings and oblations as prescribed by law, and many assumed that when they had done so all righteousness had been fulfilled. Meanwhile, dishonesty in the marketplace, perversion of justice in the courts, exploitation of the poor, and neglect of the needy were tacitly tolerated. But "iniquity and solemn assembly" are incompatible. These two can never be reconciled. God will not accept burnt offerings in lieu of justice, mercy, and obedience. Faithfulness in tithing mint, dill, and cummin cannot take the place of the weightier matters of the law.

If the record were not so clear, it would be difficult to believe that the gospel—which stresses faith, trust, obedience, mercy, and kindness—could have been supplanted by the kind of immoral religiosity that characterized the medieval period. Virtually every form of iniquity appears to have been tolerated. Then when the Western church made it possible for men to purchase indulgences for sins contemplated as well as sins committed, it was the church itself that in effect made common cause with evil. It was this practice in particular that aroused the moral indignation of Luther and others, and so sparked the Reformation.

It is the glory of Protestant Christianity that it has exalted the ethical; sometimes perhaps at the expense of the ceremonial. The radical Anabaptists, for instance, dealt all too ruthlessly with valid media of worship. Priceless treasures of religious art were destroyed; sanctuaries were stripped of all ornamentation; emotionalism supplanted the beauty of holiness. By and large, however, the Reformers were not anti-cultus. Luther abolished only those practices in public worship that were definitely contrary to the Scriptures. In the tracts and treatises of the Reformation, one finds numerous references to Word and sacrament which indicate that these were of equal importance. If, in the practice of the church, the Word came to have greater prominence than the sacrament, this must be attributed primarily to the fact that preaching had been far too long neglected. The spoken Word was deemed necessary, on the one hand, to interpret and to safeguard the original intent of the Lord's Supper and, on the other, to restore the moral life of the Christian community to a semblance of robust health.

Protestant Christianity stands on solid ground when it exalts the spoken Word. The command to teach and preach is every bit as explicit in the New Testament as the command to baptize and to observe the Lord's Supper. Strictly cultual matters in the life of the apostolic church received relatively little attention in the letters addressed to the churches. The emphasis there is on what a Christian is to be and to do. Jesus said: "Not every one who says to me, 'Lord, Lord,' shall enter the kingdom of heaven, but he who does the will of my Father who is in heaven" (Matt. 7:21). When Paul enjoined the Christians at Philippi to have the mind of Christ among themselves, he stressed humility and obedience (Phil. 2:5-11) in particular. His letters exhort Christians to walk worthily of their high calling at all times (Eph. 4:1). It is specifically pointed out that scripture is profitable "for teaching, for reproof, for correction, and for training in righteousness, that the man of God may be complete, equipped for every good work" (2 Tim. 3:17). To the credit of Protestant Christianity, it can be said that it has taken seriously the mandate to teach, to reprove, to correct, and to train in righteousness. In so doing it has made a major contribution to the moral health of the nations.

It must be admitted, however, that at times Protestant Christianity has concentrated on the ethical to the neglect of worship. In some quarters liturgical form received scant attention; at times it has been treated with roughly as much disdain as theology. Earlier some churchmen—not all, to be sure—used to boast that they knew little theology and cared less; they were concerned solely about religion and its application to life. Unfortunately, all too often this religious-ethical concern spent its force on puritanical trivialities and in so doing fostered a type of Pharisaic legalism as deadly as ceremonialism. All things considered, however, Protestant Christianity succeeded in fostering a moral earnestness, limited though this was to private morality. The danger of cere monialism, therefore, was remote. It is not, however, as remot as it was in the past.

TRACES OF SACERDOTALISM

With the liturgical renaissance, traces of ceremonialism as wel as sacerdotalism have appeared on the Protestant horizon. Som of these may have their seat in clerical pretensions, or possibl in clerical insecurity, rather than in liturgical presuppositions Along with donning clerical vestments suggesting the priestl office, ministers often adopt or acquire a tone of voice most aptl characterized as pontifical or sepulchral. By voice and variou mannerisms the impression is given that the rite of ordinatior has invested the cleric with powers and prerogatives that a laymar does not possess. What is overlooked by those who lend encourage ment to this notion is the fact that the New Testament leaves no room for sacerdotalism of any kind.

It is of more than passing significance that when the apostl Paul enumerates Christ's gifts to the church, priests are no mentioned. In Ephesians 4:11, the listing of workers in the church includes apostles, prophets, evangelists, pastors, anc teachers; in 1 Corinthians 12:28, the apostle Paul adds to this lis by including workers of miracles, healers, helpers, administrators and speakers in various kinds of tongues. When the same subjec comes up in Romans 12:6-8, the gifts distributed in the church are spelled out primarily in terms of Christian service: contrib uting with liberality, giving aid with zeal, and showing mercy with cheerfulness. Except for references to Christ as the all sufficient High Priest in the letter to the Hebrews and to the priesthood of all believers in the first letter of Peter, the New Testament maintains complete silence regarding priests and the priestly office. This, we may be sure, is not an accidental omission. Priests are not mentioned because a sacerdotal cult had become superfluous. The Christian church had no need of a priesthood invested with special powers to bridge the gap between sinful man and a holy God.

On this score the letter to the Hebrews is most forthright. Whether the author was merely trying to establish the superiority of the new covenant in comparison with the old or whether he saw a new sacerdotal cult in the making cannot be determined; but what is unmistakably clear is his conviction that a sacrificial cult, like that of the temple, had not only become obsolete and unnecessary but would, in fact, constitute a denial of the one all-sufficient offering that Christ had brought when he offered himself. As if he anticipated what later was to become the official position of Roman Catholicism regarding the mass, the writer declared: "Nor was it to offer himself repeatedly, as the high priest enters the Holy Place yearly with blood not his own; for then he would have had to suffer repeatedly since the foundation of the world. But as it is, he has appeared once for all at the end of the age to put away sin by the sacrifice of himself" (Heb. 9:25-26).

Now the New Testament does speak of the priesthood of believers which has an entirely different function from the one associated with the Old Testament or Roman priesthood. The Roman priesthood, not unlike the Aaronic order in Judaism, is set apart and invested with a unique power to serve as an intermediary between man and God. Undoubtedly there are occasions when a timid or troubled person is in need of an intermediary, but not of one who is such by virtue of his office. The New Testament doctrine of the priesthood of all believers precludes a special priesthood with a unique status before God. Every member of the Christian fellowship is to be a priest to his fellow members—not only in the sense of being an intercessor but also in the sense of being concerned about their total well-being. A Christian's role as priest is aptly summed up in the admonition: "Bear one another's burdens, and so fulfill the law of Christ" (Gal. 6:2).

The rediscovery of this New Testament principle of the priesthood of all believers undercuts any and all priestly pretensions on the part of the clergy, whether overt or covert. Luther declared in his *Appeal to the German Nobility* that anyone who has been baptized may consider himself a priest, bishop, or pope, though it would not be seemly for everyone to exercise these offices.[5] To make sure that no minister would arrogate to himself any priestly authority, John Calvin modified Bucer's *Strasbourg Liturgy* at the one place where this temptation might most easily assert itself. He substituted a prayer of pardon for the pronouncement of absolution. Though it is true that the absolution formula "I declare unto you . . . the forgiveness of all your sins" is usually introduced by the qualifying clause "by the authority of the Word of God" or "in the name of Christ," it nevertheless carries sacerdotal overtones, at least as far as the laity is concerned. And, if by chance, the declaration is made with a solemn, sonorous voice, accompanied by the sign of the cross, sacerdotal overtones become accepted facts.

To avoid any misconceptions about priestly power or authority, it is far better to couch the assurance of pardon in words of scripture which set forth the promises of God delivered through his prophets and spoken by his Son. To be sure, scripture can be cited (Matt. 16:19; John 20:23) in support of a declaration of absolution, but it is generally agreed that the keys of the kingdom—if there are such—were entrusted to the church, not to an order within the church. Moreover, a prayer of pardon is more in keeping with the mind of Christ and the practice of the apostolic church. In short, every precaution should be taken against sacerdotalism's gaining a secure foothold in the tradition of Protestant Christianity.

vi · WORSHIP AND
THE MIND OF CHRIST

In all matters of faith and morals Paul's admonition to the Christians in Philippi is regarded to be definitive: "Have this mind among yourselves, which you have in Christ Jesus" (Phil. 2:5). Every theological doctrine, every ethical principle is to be tested by the mind of Christ. Christ's mind is the criterion of the church's cultus as well. The first and foremost requirement of Christian worship is that it conform to the spirit of Jesus. Within the broad framework of Christ's spirit there is ample room for a variety of liturgical forms and practices. According to Paul, "where the Spirit of the Lord is, there is freedom" (2 Cor. 3:17). As far as we know Jesus did not lay down any hard and fast rules as to how men should worship. His basic concern appears to have been that men should worship God in spirit and in truth.

Tacitly, the mind of Christ is recognized to be normative every time a service of worship is begun with the solemn declaration, "In the name of the Father, and of the Son, and of the

Holy Spirit"; likewise every time a prayer is offered "in Jesus' name" or "through Jesus Christ our Lord." Admittedly, these phrases do not mean much, if anything, to many people. Constant usage has made them largely innocuous. At best, these and similar phrases are looked upon as a hallowed liturgical custom; at worst, they are looked upon as a kind of religious incantation or pious formula to insure the prayer's acceptability. Such notions obviously betray religious naïveté and fail to comprehend the basic intent that underlies the custom of using the name of Jesus.

When a service of worship is begun in the name of the triune God, the congregation is thereby enjoined to approach God in a spirit of reverence consonant with his will as revealed in Jesus Christ. To offer prayer in the name of Jesus Christ or through Jesus Christ means nothing unless the prayer is in harmony with Christ's spirit. Name and spirit in biblical usage have very much in common. Unless prayer reflects the sincerity, trust, humility, and obedience that characterized the life of Jesus, it is not prayer in his name, no matter how frequently his name is used or invoked. In short, to pray in Jesus' name means to acknowledge that his relationship to the heavenly Father is definitive for our relationship to God. Anything less than this is a misuse of Christ's name.

The moment we make the mind of Christ the touchstone, whether of theology, ethics, or of the church's cultus, we must at least in passing take account of a major theological question of our time. It is this: Are we sure that we can know the mind of Christ? At one time this question was answered with an unequivocal yes. Today the answer is apt to be hedged with some qualifications. The exponents of radical form criticism contend that the only Jesus we can know is the Jesus of the early church's preaching. This is to say, that in the four Gospels there is not so much a running account of what Jesus said and did as a running commentary on what he said and did. That running commentary was considerably overlaid with what, in German, is called *Gemeindetheologie,* the theologizing of the early church. Therefore, it could be claimed that far from having the original words of Jesus, and through them a look into his mind, we have the colored or biased interpretation of his followers as they understood his words and deeds. Supposedly, then, we see him only as those first interpreters saw him.

Conceivably these interpreters, who had been eyewitnesses, may have been somewhat overzealous at some points, yet, if we take their words at face value, they were scrupulously meticulous. The first epistle of John begins with the declaration: "That which was from the beginning, which we have heard, which we have seen with our eyes, which we have looked upon and touched with our hands, concerning the word of life . . . we proclaim also to you" (1 John 1:1-3). Luke assured his friend Theophilus that he was writing an orderly account of those things that had been delivered from the beginning by eyewitnesses and ministers of the word.

It is safe to say that the most radical conclusions of form criticism are not apt to stand the test of time. The renewed quest for the historical Jesus, now well under way, has already shown some of the left-wing claims to be untenable. But even if the major conclusions should be accepted at face value, a reasonably reliable image of the mind of Jesus would still emerge. Even though the preaching of the early church did have a tendency to see the fulfillment of Old Testament prophecies in almost every facet of Jesus' life and ministry, it is nevertheless true that his philosophy of work and worship shaped the thought of those who interpreted him. To assume that the apostolic community created a completely mythological Jesus stretches credulity beyond the breaking point.

This is not to claim that there were no mythologizing tendencies at work in the apostolic period. Overzealous believers attempted to make the life of Jesus more dramatic, more marvelous, more mysterious and mystifying than it really was. By way of illustration one need only compare the noncanonical gospels with the four canonical Gospels. The former glamorized the life of Jesus to the point of including miraculous deeds that Jesus repeatedly refused to perform. Generally, the Gospel writers exercised remarkable restraint in recording the things that eyewitnesses said Jesus had done. Even the nativity stories in Matthew and Luke are models of restraint.

THE RISE OF A CHRIST CULTUS

Quite a different chapter was written after the close of the apostolic period. After that there occurred what might be called a "Christ cultus" in the making. That cultus appears to have been more intent on magnifying the sacrifice of Christ than on emulating the mind of Christ. Beginning with Hippolytus, on whose liturgy all subsequent liturgies were based, down to Ambrose and Augustine in the West and Basil and Gregory in the East, the eucharistic liturgy became increasingly occult in content and ostentatious in form. By way of introducing a simple Christology Paul had said, "Great indeed, we confess, is the mystery of our religion" (1 Tim. 3:16); the liturgies of later centuries made the mystery of the Christ-event even more mysterious and mystifying, commendable as the underlying intent may have been.

Both Eastern Orthodox and Roman Catholic liturgies can be cited as a case in point. The Eastern Orthodox liturgies—and there are several—have been described by Horton Davies as "a holy drama taking place in heaven and on earth,"[1] the focal point being the mystery of the incarnation. The effect of these liturgies is that of intensifying the mystery of the Christ-event.

The first part of the service, for example, is conducted in secret behind a screen, called an iconostasis. All action at this time is hidden from the worshipers' view; even the prayers are offered silently. When the action is brought into view, every posture and movement is highly symbolical. This is particularly true of the two processions known as the Great Entrance and the Little Entrance. From the Protestant perspective the entire service is unduly encumbered with liturgical symbolism.

Much the same can be said about the Roman mass, which is basically a celebration of the atonement. Its intent is to re-present Christ's sacrifice on the cross by a bloodless sacrifice enacted on the altar. The ceremonial splendor surrounding this act is, however, a far cry from the gruesome event that occurred on Calvary. It is also in sharp contrast to the plain ceremonial meal shared by Jesus and his disciples in the Upper Room. Karl Barth is reported by Donald Baillie to have said: "The mass in its conception, content, and construction is a religious masterpiece."[2] But this, Barth points out, is also its weakness. Religious art is one thing, obedience to Christ is something else.

All this raises the question whether the laudable intent to honor Christ did not give way to a Christ cult that became less harmonious with the mind of Christ as it became progressively more elaborate. Does an elaborate liturgy—whether Eastern Orthodox, Roman Catholic, Anglican, Lutheran, or any other designed to magnify the name of the crucified and risen Lord—really reflect the mind of the Lord? Is it possible that Christ is dishonored by the very ceremonial pomp and pageantry that are supposed to exalt him? Within Roman Catholicism serious questions have been raised concerning the regal splendor of the vestments worn by bishops, archbishops, and cardinals. That question may well be raised, for there is something patently incongruous between the "soft raiment" worn by Christ's vicars and the son of man who had "nowhere to lay his head" (Matt. 8:20).

Clerical splendor is a relatively minor issue when it comes to bringing the Christ cult of the church into line with the mind of Christ. Every liturgy, Protestant as well as Roman Catholic and Eastern Orthodox, needs to be measured by our Lord's precepts and example. Meet and proper as it is for the church to exalt the crucified and risen Lord, whose name is above every other name, it is even more important that his spirit be emulated in the work and worship of the church. "Why do you call me 'Lord, Lord,' and not do what I tell you?" (Luke 6:46) is a question that cannot be ignored. Will the Lord of life be pleased if liturgical splendor should inadvertently become an end in itself and take the place of his humility and obedience?

For similar reasons one is constrained to raise serious questions about a rising Virgin Mary cult within Protestant Christianity.[3] Prominent Protestant theologians appear to be moving toward a rapprochement with Roman Catholicism regarding the status of the mother of Jesus. Protestants are warned against a totally negative "Marian minimalism." Various reasons on biblical and ecclesiological grounds are given for reevaluating the status of Mary. What may be the result of this endeavor is difficult to predict. Should it gain momentum it will certainly be introduced into the cultus of the church. But let the church beware lest a cultic practice, however noble in conception, be found wanting when tested by the mind of Christ. This could easily prove to be a cultic enrichment without either a biblical or an ethical foundation.

THE MIND OF CHRIST

On the basis of the Gospel record, and supporting evidence in the Epistles, it can be stated that Jesus stood squarely within the prophetic tradition by doing the will of God. This does not mean that he was indifferent about faithfulness in cultic matters. We know that he attended the synagogue on the sabbath day, but to what extent he met the ceremonial requirements prescribed in the Levitical code is unknown. Whether he ever had occasion to take issue with the temple cult, aside from the one time when he drove the traders and money changers from the temple, is also unknown. But it is significant that the chief priests spearheaded the conspiracy that led to his crucifixion. Since it is not likely that this one episode could have generated the deep-seated animosity that the hierarchy appears to have had, it must be assumed that on previous occasions Jesus had been as forthright in denouncing ceremonialism as he was in denouncing legalism. Evidences of the latter are found throughout the Gospels. Fasting, tithing, heaping up empty phrases in prayer, punctiliousness in matters of sabbath observance, and similar puritanical practices all came under his righteous wrath.

More important than Jesus' critical attitude toward ceremonialism and legalism is his emphasis on doing the will of God. That is the dominant motif of his mission. "My food," he said, "is to do the will of him who sent me, and to accomplish his work" (John 4:34). The manner in which he met the three temptations (Matt. 4:1-11) at the beginning of his ministry underscores this determination. His steadfastness in going to Jerusalem in spite of the known hazards and the dissuasive efforts of his disciples fully confirms it. Even if the Gospels did not contain any overt references of his commitment to the will of God, the overall impact of his life and ministry would still compel us to concur with Paul when, in his Christology (Phil. 2:5-11), he lifted up humility and obedience as the hallmarks of the mind of Christ.

What Christ exemplified in his own life he expected of his followers. As the record shows, Jesus said very little about worship as such. The few references to cultic practices, such as fasting, praying, and offering gifts at the altar, are predominantly ethical in character, not cultic. This should not escape our attention. Evidence supporting this claim is found in the collection of teachings commonly called the Sermon on the Mount. Consistently the emphasis is placed on what a man is and what he does. Particularly pointed are the references to the sound tree that bears good fruit and to the wise man who builds his house on the rock. God recognizes men, not by what they say, no matter how effusive their "Lord's, Lord's" may be, but by what they do (Matt. 7:15-27). John Calvin may not have intended to give a summation of the mind of Christ, but he came very close to doing so when he declared, "True worship consists in obedience alone."[4]

Calvin did not mean that there is no place for public worship, nor that we can dispense with all liturgical aids to worship. However, apart from obedience and similar attitudes of heart and mind, worship is a noisy gong and a clanging cymbal. For this reason churches in the Reformed tradition have always placed great emphasis on the preaching of the Word. This is not because there is anything sacrosanct about preaching in itself, but because "the Word of God is living and active, sharper than any two-edged sword" (Heb. 4:12). When the Word is proclaimed with some degree of competence and conviction, believers are not apt to forget that their primary responsibility is to honor God with their lives, and not just with their lips.

Not to be forgotten either is the importance of hymnody. Hymn singing may fall far short of its purpose; this can readily happen. Not only are hymns sung listlessly, but what is more serious, too little attention is paid to the words. Yet their message may come through more often than anyone dares to assume. Be that as it may, hymns have the added advantage of being couched in poetic language of singular appeal; they also speak with a voice of lofty anonymity in contrast to the "thus saith" of the preacher, whose diction may be poor and whose tone may be moralistic. Hymns chosen with an eye to supplementing the scripture reading and sermon can add meaningfully to the worship of God.

There is another facet of the mind of Christ that has bearing on worship. It is best described by such words as naturalness, artlessness, intimacy, sincerity. Artlessness is defined as "free from artificiality" or "free from guile or craft." Our Lord's relationship to God stands out in this respect. If his humanity is taken seriously, as it should be, this quality of his devotional life is most significant. He spoke to his heavenly Father in the manner that children speak to their parents; that is, without formality, inhibitions, pretensions, or abject obeisance.

Again it must be said, what Jesus exemplified in his relationship to God he encouraged his followers to emulate in their approach to God. They were to ask, to seek, to knock, on the assumption that the heavenly Father is ready to "give good gifts to those who ask him." No special formality need be observed beyond that of trust and respect normal to a healthy, wholesome parent-child relationship. He declared prayer to be as natural and simple as entering a room, closing the door, and speaking to the Father who is in secret.

The fact that his disciples had to ask him to teach them how to pray—before he offered what is known to us as the Lord's Prayer—is also significant. Of course, no one may presume to read the mind of the Master on this matter, but one might hazard the guess that he had refrained from giving his disciples a specific prayer on the premise that anything like a prescribed prayer tends to become formal, even acquiring an intrinsic sacredness. That is the case when each counted bead of a rosary is considered to be a paternoster or when Protestants open or close a church meeting by "reciting" the Lord's Prayer. His prayer is too rich in content and too broad in compass to be reduced to the level of a talisman.

Noteworthy, too, is the simple salutation with which the prayer begins: "Our Father." This suggests not only that one can trust in God but also that God need not be addressed with high-flown references to his majesty and mercy, either to attract his attention or to gain his favor. If, on the one hand, this can be interpreted to mean that God does not insist on proper protocol, it can also be interpreted to mean that man does not need to abase himself as though he were nothing more than a "miserable worm." There was a time when language of this kind was common coinage in the church. Whether it contributed anything toward fostering genuine humility is difficult to judge. Perhaps the pendulum has now swung too far in the other direction.

Possibly this may be one reason why questions have been raised regarding the term miserable offenders in the prayer of general confession. Compared with the prodigal's confession: "Father, I have sinned against heaven and before you; I am no longer worthy to be called your son" (Luke 15:21), the term may seem to claim too much. The prodigal's confession, as Jesus phrased it in the parable, says all that needs to be said. It is free of what might be called exaggerated self-abasement. God knows our sins and shortcomings all too well; it is not necessary for us to catalog them in lurid terms. By way of contrast, the general confession, "We have left undone those things which we ought to have done; and we have done those things which we ought not to have done," is remarkably apt, largely because it does not say too much. Every worshiper can enumerate his own particular sins of omission and commission. One could argue, of course, that this confession is too vague and general to be meaningful; nevertheless, in this instance the very lack of specificity is a greater asset than liability.

A reservation might also be registered concerning a question included in some baptismal formulas. Parents and sponsors are asked: "Do you renounce the vain pomp and glory of the world, the lust of the flesh, and all evil works and ways?"[5] They are expected to reply, "I do." Well might they ask, however: What is the vain pomp and glory of the world? What is the lust of the flesh, and all evil works and ways? Who may presume to say at what precise point the legitimate enjoyment of God's bounty becomes idolatrous hedonism? Moreover, considering the fact that worldliness, even if not worldly pomp and glory, can be found under the monk's cowl as well as in the millionaire's mansion, parents might even question a cleric's right to exact of them a promise that only a completely dedicated ascetic may venture to make. The plea here is not that the responsibilities of the baptismal covenant should be treated lightly or made easy; on the contrary, they should be taken with utmost seriousness. But extravagant promises made under the duress of a liturgical form subtract from rather than add to the seriousness of the baptismal covenant.

To encumber any act of public worship with declarations of abject self-debasement or with extravagant professions of loyalty runs counter to the mind of Christ. If it is said that Jesus never minimized the cost of discipleship, it should also be said that he never equated the cost of discipleship with effusive protestations of piety such as those reflected in the prayer of the Pharisee (Luke 18:11-12). What the Pharisee's prayer reveals is an exaggerated pose of piety, condemned alike by its pretensions and its profuseness. The publican's prayer, on the other hand, is a model of sincerity, void of any feigned humility or contrived contrition. It is in line with what Jesus said about becoming as little children in order to enter the kingdom. While it would be presumptuous to equate his conception of childlikeness with sincerity or artlessness, it is certain that these are included.

Such qualities are by no means exclusively a matter of liturgical form. The childlike artlessness that is void of affectation and artificiality is dependent fully as much upon the liturgist as the liturgy. Personal observations and experiences as a guest preacher in many pulpits have brought this home to me with frightening forcefulness; perhaps never so compellingly as on the two occasions when I preached in Anglican churches in Great Britain. Except for minor modifications the liturgy was the same in both instances, but what a marked difference in the way the liturgy was conducted. In the one instance, the congregation was led in worship without any pontifical pretensions; in the other, an aura of artificiality hovered over the service from beginning to end.

We have been saying that worship, in keeping with the mind of Christ, is to be free of everything contrived to impress either God or man. Measured by this same standard of Christ's mind, worship is also basically simple—simple in the sense of being free of liturgical and theological complexities. Much has been said and written, and rightly so, about the simplicity that was in Christ. It is recorded that the common people heard him gladly. Certainly one reason for this was the fact that they understood what he said. He used simple language and employed picturesque parables to set forth the nature of the kingdom of God. The scribes, Pharisees, and Sadducees understood him too—so well, in fact, that they were enraged by what he said. Jesus had a way of piercing their finespun legalistic theorizing to reach the heart of what Moses and the prophets had said. There is one thing that is unmistakably clear about the mind of Christ: it did not move in the ontological stratosphere of metaphysical abstraction. In Jesus we are confronted by what Samuel H. Miller has aptly called "the amazing simplicity of a profound faith."

Several references in the Gospels might suggest that the parables of Jesus were not generally understood. Even the disciples were perplexed. Mark (4:10-13, 33-34) reports that the twelve asked him about the meaning of what he had said concerning the seed that fell on four different kinds of soil. The interpretation that Jesus gave is prefaced with the comment, "To you has been given the secret of the kingdom of God, but for those outside everything is in parables; so that they may indeed see but not perceive, and may indeed hear but not understand; lest they should turn again, and be forgiven" (Mark 4:11-12). One does not need to accept all the claims of form criticism to recognize in this observation some gratuitous theologizing imposed upon the parable, either to enhance the authority of the apostles or to give the parables an unwarranted aura of mystery. A similar reference is found in the Fourth Gospel. The disciples are reported to have said: "Ah, now you are speaking plainly, not in any figure! Now we know that you know all things, and need none to question you; by this we believe you came from God" (John 16:29-30). This, too, has all the earmarks of an unwarranted editorial comment. The teachings of Jesus are remarkably free of theological subtleties intended to obscure the truth or perplex the listener.

It is important to distinguish between profundity and abstruseness, between simplicity and shallowness. Jesus probed the depths of reality with unparalleled clarity and incisiveness. He displayed a singular ability to say profound things in simple terms. There is no evidence at hand to suggest that he ever sought to mystify or confuse his listeners. He was no devotee of the cult of the unintelligible. Nor is there any evidence at hand to suggest that he associated worship with something esoteric or occult. When the woman of Samaria confessed her perplexity about the right place to worship, he declared this question to be irrelevant by pointing out that "true worshipers will worship the Father in spirit and truth" (John 4:23).

Worship, beyond a doubt, is as profound a human act as any aspiration or experience can be. It springs from the very core of our being and penetrates the realm of ultimate reality as far as human finitude permits. Yet worship is not a complex or complicated act. It need not be encumbered with recondite symbolism or intricate, involved theological thought. If so, millions of ordinary people who are unaware of all the delicate nuances that liturgiologists and theologians have either imposed upon the cultus or read into it, do not really worship. For the average person in the pew, worship is the simple act of recognizing with humility and gratitude the unmerited goodness and grace of God. If anything is found wanting in his worship it is more apt to be the lack of wholeheartedness. Liturgical naïveté does not stand in his way of giving to God the honor and glory due unto his name.

That there is considerable liturgical naïveté abroad in the church is obvious, possibly even among those who have become disciples of liturgical reform. Much of this may well be inexcusable. On the other hand, the theological subtleties that have been imposed on the cultus of the church are mixed blessings, to say the least. Reference has already been made to the mystifying effect of the Orthodox liturgy and the Roman mass. A liturgy serves no useful purpose unless it is understood. Let it not be assumed, however, that every facet of the Protestant cultus is completely above criticism.

Consider, for instance, the prayer of consecration in the liturgy of the Lord's Supper. In some quarters this prayer has been invested with a symbolic significance far different from that which Jesus associated with the ritual of giving thanks before breaking the bread and taking the cup. Biblical scholars are generally in agreement that Jesus, in keeping with Hebrew tradition, did not invoke a special blessing *upon* the loaf and cup, but gave thanks to God *for* all his gifts as symbolized by the loaf and cup. The eucharistic prayer found in some denominational manuals of worship appears to have a different intent. The petition in question speaks for itself. "We most humbly beseech thee to send down thy Holy Spirit to sanctify both us and these thine own gifts of bread and wine . . . , that the bread which we break may be the communion of the body of Christ, and the cup of blessing which we bless, the communion of the blood of Christ."[6] The language of the eucharistic invocation in the *Book of Common Prayer* is quite similar. "We most humbly beseech thee, O merciful Father . . . to bless and sanctify, with thy Word and Holy Spirit, these thy gifts and creatures of bread and wine." In both instances the petition is more than a prayer of thanksgiving for the elements; in effect this is a consecration of the elements, commonly referred to as the epiclesis. As such it carries faint overtones of transubstantiation for which there is no Upper Room precedent. What Jesus did when he took the bread and the cup and gave thanks had no other ritualistic meaning than to acknowledge God as the giver of every good and perfect gift.

Much to the concern of many lay people and clergy, the Lord's Supper is sometimes celebrated with an elaborate ritual that tends to obscure its basic purpose of remembering and proclaiming the Lord's death and of anticipating his ultimate triumph. In saying this, the basic intent of the eucharistic liturgy is not called into question. The liturgy was designed to make the act of coming to the Lord's table a meaningful occasion. This can be taken for granted. Nevertheless, the question must be raised whether the very richness of the liturgy with its glorias, Te Deums, confessions, and intercessions may attract so much attention to itself that communicants eat of the bread and drink of the cup "without discerning the body," to use a phrase of the apostle Paul.

This does not suggest that the church should return to the relatively simple, ceremonially unencumbered celebration of the Eucharist in apostolic times. This is neither possible nor desirable. It is important, however, that the church retain or recapture that personal intimacy with the crucified and risen Lord of which the early church was so keenly aware. It may be instructive at this point to recall that whenever the cultus of the church has become unduly elaborate, and simultaneously very formal as well, sectarian movements have sprung up. In due time most of these have in turn become formidable denominations with well-developed cultic forms and customs, usually far more elaborate than the first dissenters would have tolerated. If the present liturgical renaissance continues to move toward more symbolism, more litanies, and the like, then the time will surely come when the descendants of the present cultic reformers will in turn become the progenitors of reformers who will simplify the cultus for the sake of spiritual vitality. Liturgy, like theology, can become more complicated than it needs to be. When it does, true piety has a way of breaking through whatever forms and fetters liturgical embellishments have imposed upon the cultus.

In all fairness it must be said, however, that sometimes liturgical embellishments are the product of theological ideas. Just as one can speak of a liturgical subversion of theology, so one can also speak of a theological subversion of liturgy. The transition from the apostolic conception of the Eucharist to the Roman mass is a case in point. Without some theological support, it is unlikely that the observance of the Eucharist could have become so sacerdotal in such a short time. A review of the theological treatises of the first five or six centuries reveals very clearly that except for the Augustinian concept of Christ's presence in the Eucharist, which leaned toward a dynamic spiritual presence, the realistic metabolism of the Ambrosian school of thought would have become official theology long before it did. So theology gives shape to the liturgy.

And it continues to do so. The current trend toward more liturgy is at least partially theologically based. We are reminded that the liturgy should be a re-presentation of the Christ-event.

Joseph Sittler is of the same opinion when he says "to be a Christian is to have one's life in its shape determined by the shape of what God has done." And the shape of what God has done is presumably to be set forth in the Lord's day liturgy. Dr. Sittler continues: "The morphology of grace in the life, death, resurrection, and exaltation of Jesus Christ imparts to and creates in the believer its own shape—so worship is the celebration of this new being in Christ by his body, the church."[7] Does the implementation of this principle call for the dramatic and esoteric symbolism of an Orthodox liturgy? If so, Frederick Herzog is certainly right when he insists that "Christian worship . . . makes sense only if every symbolic act is permeated by an adequate understanding of the basic datum to which it refers."[8]

Is the liturgical renaissance moving in the direction of impregnating the liturgy with so many subtle theological nuances that the Word which "became flesh and dwelt among us, full of grace and truth" (John 1:14), will become veiled? When Paul compared the old covenant with the new, he spoke of Moses' putting "a veil over his face so that the Israelites might not see the end of the fading splendor" (2 Cor. 3:12). And then, with an obvious reference to Jews who had not accepted Christ, he continues: "Yes, to this day whenever Moses is read a veil lies over their minds" (2 Cor. 3:15). Was the veil only over their minds, or was it over the old covenant as well? The words that follow suggest that the old covenant was also at fault, for we read, "when a man turns to the Lord the veil is removed" (2 Cor. 3:16). The cultus can become veiled, too, or cause the minds of men to become veiled. The cultus can become so elaborate, so rigid and formal, so mysterious and mystifying that the simplicity of worship is sacrificed on the altar of theological sophistication and liturgical splendor. So much attention can be given to liturgical minutiae that there is an impeding of the soul's quest for the living God, who "in these last days . . . has spoken to us by a Son, whom he appointed the heir of all things, through whom also he created the world" (Heb. 1:2).

vii · THE EUCHARIST:
ITS ORIGIN AND OBSERVANCE

Throughout its long history the Christian church has always regarded the celebration of the Eucharist to be the innermost sanctuary of the whole Christian worship. Several exceptions to this consensus are to be noted however. The Quakers, for instance, observe neither baptism nor the Lord's Supper; not because they are anti-sacramental but because they believe that an external rite cannot contribute anything to what is basically an internal, spiritual relationship. Churches that stand in the extreme liberal tradition are also exceptions to the general rule. A good case might even be made for the claim that Protestant Christianity has not accorded the sacrament of Holy Communion the importance it has given to the Word. The Reformers stressed the equality and the inseparability of Word and sacrament, yet in practice both they and their spiritual heirs appear to have exalted the Word at the expense of the sacrament. The question of whether the Eucharist has been given the prominence it deserves cannot be decided solely on the basis of the frequency or infrequency of its observance. To apply this as a standard of measurement would be misleading and unwarranted. When the broad sweep of church history is reviewed, ample evidence comes to light suggesting that Protestants in general have maintained a high view regarding the uniqueness, the centrality, the sacredness of the Eucharist. Its identification with the great festivals of the church year might be cited as supporting evidence.

Relatively early in the church's history, the Liturgy of the Word was absorbed in the Liturgy of the Upper Room. Preaching then became a lost art and the instruction of the young in the rich lore of the Hebrew-Christian tradition was sadly neglected. In the medieval period even the priesthood was to a large extent too illiterate to read anything except the mass. Basically, worship in both East and West meant celebrating the mass or its equivalent. Every phase and facet of the liturgy pointed toward that supreme moment when the elements of bread and wine were consecrated and offered to God as an oblation, either in gratitude or in penitence. Many people deemed worship to be complete if one had witnessed the elevation of the Host. Having been present for that moment, they could be on their way, fully convinced that all righteousness had been fulfilled.

The writings of the ante-Nicene and post-Nicene Fathers bear witness to the fact that the foremost theologians from the beginning of the second century to the Fourth Lateran Council (1215) were not only engaged in combating heresy but also in developing a theology of the Eucharist. With the Reformation came another radical reorientation of the church's understanding of the Eucharist. It was then that virtually all sacerdotal elements associated with the mass were set aside as being contrary to the Scriptures.

Today the ecumenical movement has brought to the surface the deep cleavages within Christendom regarding the Lord's Supper. Even within the membership of the World Council of Churches there are wide differences of doctrine regarding this sacrament. So profound are these differences that Anglicans, Eastern Orthodox, and Lutherans have not been able to join their fellow Christians of the various Protestant bodies at the Lord's table. The dilemma in which the churches find themselves at this point has given momentum to a fresh study of the nature of the Eucharist. If the differences that separate the churches could be resolved by theological and biblical studies alone, the day would not be too distant when all members of the World Council of Churches could break the bread and share the cup together, for the study of the Eucharist is the center of current theological inquiry. However, penitence may be just as necessary as study and research, and ecumenically minded churchmen have not hesitated to say so.

So many scholarly books and articles dealing with the Eucharist have appeared in recent decades that it seems presumptuous to attempt to add anything to what has already been well said. These final chapters on the subject are included primarily for the purpose of recording a point of view that is based not so much on the tradition and practice of the churches, whether ancient or modern, as on the New Testament data concerning the Lord's Supper. Both the words of institution spoken in the Upper Room and the practice of the church in the apostolic period are taken into account.

THE BIBLICAL SETTING

Until approximately the beginning of the present century, it was generally assumed that Jesus instituted the Lord's Supper in connection with the observance of the Jewish Passover. All three synoptic Gospels are explicit in stating that Jesus sent several of the disciples to "go and prepare the passover for us, that we may eat it" (Luke 22:8). When the preparations had been made in the place identified only as the Upper Room, Jesus and the twelve met there "when it was evening" (Mark 14:17). Beyond this no further mention is made of the Passover, save that Luke reports Jesus as saying: "I have earnestly desired to eat this passover with you before I suffer" (Luke 22:15). It must be remembered that by the time the Gospels were written the observance of the Eucharist had become the one distinctive facet of the Christian cultus. Whatever interest the Christian community may have had in the Jewish Passover was strictly academic. Furthermore, there is the possibility that the synoptic account reflects fully as much the established practice of the church as a verbatim report of what transpired in the Upper Room.

More recently many scholars have come to regard the Jewish kiddush as the more likely setting of the Last Supper. A kiddush was a quasi-religious meal that a small company of friends, called a *haburah,* observed on the eve of a sabbath or a feast day. The meal on these occasions appears to have been relatively simple, the emphasis being on fellowship rather than on food. Normally the leader of the group acted as host.

A kiddush derived its ceremonial significance from the blessings that were spoken over the food before eating. The so-called blessing over the bread and the cup was in the nature of a thanksgiving to God for his bounty. It was *not* thought of as an act of consecrating the bread and the cup. One such blessing commonly used will suffice to make this clear: "Blessed art thou, O Lord, Ruler of the universe, the One who causeth bread to spring forth from the earth." What is noteworthy here is that *God* is blessed, not the bread. The symbolism of this ritual is similar in character to the cultic action referred to in Psalm 116:13, where the poet declares that in fulfillment of his vows he "will lift up the cup of salvation and call on the name of the Lord." This blessing, not unlike that of the kiddush thanksgivings, was an acknowledgment of God's providence and steadfast love. In passing, it is worth noting that the verb bless is often used synonymously with giving thanks—as in Psalm 103, "Bless the Lord, O my soul: and all that is within me, bless his holy name!"

The arguments commonly expressed in favor of a kiddush setting as against a Passover setting include the following points. In the synoptic account no mention is made of the paschal lamb aside from the indefinite reference in Mark. He reports: "And on the first day of the week of Unleavened Bread, when they sacrificed the passover lamb, his disciples said to him, 'Where will you have us go and prepare for you to eat the passover?' " (Mark 14:12). In the above account, *they* coupled with the past tense of the verb *sacrifice* seems to refer to what the Jews generally did rather than to what the disciples were about to do. As a matter of fact, the disciples asked where they were to prepare the Passover. Missing in the synoptic account is the use of the liturgical narrative of the Passover. Furthermore, only one cup is mentioned, whereas the Passover ritual called for four. Scholars have also pointed out that it would have been most unusual if the Passover had been observed in any other way than as a family gathering with the head of the household presiding at the meal as it had been done on the eve of Israel's escape from Egypt.

Although no firm consensus has been reached as to whether the Eucharist had its setting at a Passover meal or a kiddush, the latter appears to be gaining favor. This is not to say, however, that the fundamental character of the Eucharist is in any way affected by its Hebrew point of origin. The Lord's Supper is the sign and seal of a distinctly new covenant. It may have a measure of similarity with one or the other of these two Jewish cultic rites, just as Christian baptism has points of similarity with the ablutions prescribed by the Holiness Code or with John's baptism on the banks of the Jordan. The most obvious similarity is that the Lord's Supper, like the Passover, speaks of deliverance. The Passover reminded the Jews of their deliverance from the bondage of slavery; the Lord's Supper speaks to Christians of their deliverance from the bondage of sin. Furthermore, whatever soteriological meanings the Eucharist may have had from the very outset or may have acquired in the course of time, Paul's account makes it reasonably clear that the church observed this sacrament not as the Christian counterpart of a Jewish rite, but in obedience to the Lord's command: "Do this in remembrance of me" (1 Cor. 11:24).

At this point it seems important to direct attention to the four primary New Testament sources regarding the Lord's Supper: 1 Corinthians 11:17-32; Mark 14:22-25; Matthew 26:26-29; Luke 22:14-19. Aside from minor variations or additions these four accounts are basically identical. In the main, three major motifs can be distinguished.

1. The Lord's Supper is the sign and seal of a new covenant that carries with it the assurance of God's mercy. Matthew states quite explicitly that the blood of the covenant "is poured out for many for the forgiveness of sins" (Matt. 26:28). Paul elaborates on this theme with his exhortation that a man examine himself lest he eat and drink "judgment upon himself" (1 Cor. 11:29). It can be concluded, therefore, that in both Matthew and Paul the soteriological motif is pronounced.

2. The Lord's Supper is also a memorial. Although the phrase "Do this in remembrance of me" does not occur in the synoptic Gospels, Paul's use of these words has preserved for a later day what must have been a fairly common practice in the primitive church. It underscores the fact that the early Christians observed the Lord's Supper as an act of reverently remembering all that Jesus had said and done. This is in full accord with what might be said to be the undeclared intent of the words

of institution reported in the Gospels. Jesus instituted this rite so that his followers might have something concrete by which to remember him, especially something that would remind them of his supreme sacrifice. Even after more than nineteen hundred years one can hardly come to the Lord's table without remembering, as the *Evangelical Catechism* phrases it, "how hard it was for our Savior to bear our sins and the sins of the whole world . . . by offering up his life and shedding his blood."[1]

3. The Lord's Supper also enshrines a futuristic motif. All three synoptists include a reference to a future messianic banquet in the Father's kingdom. Again Matthew is the most explicit. Jesus is heard to say: "I shall not drink again of this fruit of the vine until that day when I drink it new with you in my Father's kingdom" (Matt. 26:29). Paul included this same motif when he wrote, "For as often as you eat this bread and drink this cup, you proclaim the Lord's death until he comes" (1 Cor. 11:26). One might add that this sentence includes also the subordinate motif of looking upon the observance of the Eucharist as a form of Christian witnessing—"you proclaim the Lord's death." This motif and the one of which it is a part receive relatively little attention both in the practice of the church and in the literature dealing with the Lord's Supper.

In addition to the four accounts of the Eucharist just considered, reference must also be made to the discourse on the bread of life found in the Fourth Gospel (John 6:25-65). Following the account of the feeding of the five thousand, the Evangelist records at some length a controversial discussion between Jesus and his countrymen in the synagogue at Capernaum. At issue is the question of eating his flesh and drinking his blood. "How can this man give us his flesh to eat?" they wanted to know. The eucharistic implications of this discourse are obvious, even though no specific reference is made to the Last Supper or the cultus of the church.

This passage is important, too, because it throws light on the theological questions that had arisen in the church concerning Christology in general and the Lord's Supper in particular. The discourse underscores, first of all, the fact that at the Lord's table believers actualized for themselves the presence of the risen Lord in some very special way. This is the import of the sentence: "He who eats my flesh and drinks my blood abides in me, and I in him" (John 6:56). And those who do this "will live forever" (John 6:51). Though eating *his* flesh and drinking *his* blood is an obvious reference to Christ's sacrificial death, the emphasis is really on the presence of the risen Lord and on the life to come.

Then there is the identification of bread and wine with flesh and blood. Very likely this emphasis is due to the overall apologetic purpose of the Gospel to combat the rising heresy of Docetism. In the very first chapter the author points out that the Word, which was from the beginning and through which all things were made, is the Word that "became flesh and dwelt among us" (John 1:14). He wants it clearly understood that the Christ of experience is not to be divorced from the Jesus of history. In this discourse on the bread of life, the emphasis on flesh and blood is in line with the Gospel's polemic against the docetic tendencies that had sprung up.

It is also probable that the eucharistic practice of the church was already moving—ever so lightly, to be sure—from the metaphorical formula used by Paul in his letter to the Corinthians toward the later concept of a substantive presence in the transubstantiated bread and wine. Paul speaks of the "body which is broken for you,"[2] and of the cup of "the new covenant" (1 Cor. 11:25). Flesh and blood are not mentioned by him. Now whether or not John's Gospel is covertly moving in the direction of the later dogma of the church is open to conjecture. The language, however, is more literalistic than metaphorical. Hence, John might well have been cited at a later time to support a doctrine of transubstantiation.

Another inference to be drawn from this discourse is that eating the flesh and drinking the blood derives its validity from "the spirit that gives life; the flesh is of no avail" (John 6:63). This reflects a similarity of thought with that which is found in the Pauline account of the Eucharist. As previously noted, Paul speaks of eating and drinking in an unworthy manner. This occurs when the body of Christ is not discerned in the bread and the cup. In other words, bread and wine are not inherently efficacious. John seems to be saying this too. If on the one hand he stresses the physical flesh and blood, he is equally emphatic regarding the importance of the spiritual. Eating flesh that is not Spirit-infused has no value, for "the words that I have spoken to you are spirit and life" (John 6:63). In short, the sacrament without the Word is incomplete.

By way of summarizing the theology and the cultus of the church in the apostolic period, it is necessary to turn attention once more to Paul's account of the Eucharist in his first letter to the Corinthians. In the church at Corinth—and very likely elsewhere as well—the Eucharist was observed at the close of the agape, the love feast, as it is commonly called. Christians assembled on the first day of the week for a fellowship meal, which was concluded with the Lord's Supper. The setting was more like that of a congregational potluck dinner than a formal service of worship. Unfortunately, the love feast lent itself to gluttony and other evils, all of which detracted from a meaningful observance of the Lord's Supper. What was intended to foster Christian fellowship frequently accentuated differences and bred envy and strife. The rich made a display of their affluence instead of sharing their food with the impoverished members of the church. These abuses, which had already come to light in Paul's day, increased to such an extent that finally there was a complete separation of Eucharist and agape. The Eucharist became identified with public worship and the agape was eventually proscribed completely.

In this early period the elements of bread and wine were brought by the people. When the moment for the observance of the Eucharist had come, the bread and wine were placed on the table, the leader of the group offered a simple prayer of thanksgiving, as Jesus had done in the Upper Room, and then the elements were distributed. The prayer was one of thanksgiving and the sacrament became known as *eucharistia,* which in translation simply means thanksgiving. The bread and wine were offered to God in gratitude for his goodness and his grace. In no sense was this simple blessing thought of as an act of consecrating and infusing the elements with a quality or substance beyond that which was inherent in them. Bread was bread and wine was wine.

Compared with most eucharistic liturgies of later times, the ritual of blessing the bread and cup appears to have been simple and brief. There prevailed an atmosphere of informality to the point of disorder. In any event Paul found it necessary to insist that "all things should be done decently and in order" (1 Cor. 14:40). From the lack of order we may conclude that in this early period the church had no recognized officials, such as elders or bishops, entrusted with responsibility for the maintenance of order. The distinction between clergy and laity was still unknown.

The most important aspect of the Eucharist is the actualization of the presence of the crucified and risen Lord. In what precise manner he was understood to be present is not spelled out in any of the New Testament literature. Very likely there was no need to do so. So radiant and vibrant was the faith of the early church in the risen and exalted Lord that nothing more than the rite of remembrance, as commanded by the Lord, was necessary to visualize him as being present in their midst. One thing is certain:

Christ's presence was real—though not in any substantive or corporeal form. Christ was deemed to be present in the action of the Eucharist rather than in the elements.

Oscar Cullmann and others have pointed out that according to the primitive view, "one ate *with* Christ but did not *eat Christ*." The certainty of the resurrection was "the essential religious motive of the primitive Lord's Supper."[3] He finds it to be of more than passing significance that most of the resurrection appearances occurred while the disciples were eating. A good example is Luke's report that the two Emmaus disciples recognized him "in the breaking of the bread" (Luke 24:35). So the symbolic act of breaking the bread at the Eucharist was both a recollection of Christ's appearance to the disciples and a reproduction of it in the cultic experience of the church. "Thus the Lord's presence was re-experienced during these love feasts, both as a recollection of the *historical* fact of the resurrection and as an experience of the *contemporary* fact of his invisible coming in the gathering of Christians assembled 'to break bread.' "[4]

HISTORICAL DEVELOPMENT

A comparison of the theologically uncomplicated faith and the liturgically unadorned practice of the apostolic church with the church's faith and practice in the following centuries is illuminating and instructive. Beginning with Ignatius, who spoke of the Eucharist as the medicine of immortality, and continuing to the Fourth Lateran Council (1215), the sacrament of the Lord's Supper became increasingly freighted with theological meanings and liturgical practices unknown in the early church. A brief résumé, based on the writings of the church fathers, illustrates what happened.

The blessing spoken over the elements as an expression of gratitude for God's goodness and grace became an invocation, petitioning the Holy Spirit to descend upon the elements as well as upon the gathered fellowship. Simultaneously, the eucharistized bread and wine became first the antitype of the body of Christ (Hippolytus) and then the transubstantiated flesh and blood of Christ (Justin). The thank offering of bread and wine, brought by the worshipers for use at the Eucharist, gradually acquired a propitiatory nature and became something offered to God to atone for sin; finally it became the bloodless sacrifice of Christ on the altar in the liturgy of the mass.

What transpires on the altar is conceived to be a real sacrifice. The dogma adopted by the Council of Trent states very clearly: "The holy Synod teaches that this sacrifice is truly propitiatory." He "who offered himself on the cross" is "the same victim, now offered through the ministry of the priesthood," the only difference being "in the method of sacrifice."[5] By this time the Eucharist was fully, frankly, unreservedly sacerdotal in nature. Instead of being the sign and seal of God's grace offered freely through the redemptive death of Christ, it had become a sacrifice that the church offered anew to atone for sin.

It is no oversimplification to say that instead of man's *receiving* something in the Eucharist—namely the assurance that his sins are forgiven—he was later *doing* something so that his sins would be forgiven. More specifically stated, it is the priest who does something. In reply to the question in a Roman Catholic catechism, "Does this change of bread and wine into the body and blood of Christ continue to be made in the church?" the answer is given: "This change of bread and wine into the body and blood of Christ continues to be made in the church by Jesus Christ through the ministry of his priests."[6] This last phrase "through the ministry of his priests" is not to be overlooked.

The writings of Ignatius and Hippolytus, whose *Apostolic Tradition* was definitive for the liturgical development in both East and West, as well as those of Justin, Tertullian, Ambrose, Augustine, and others expound the theological understanding of the Eucharist with considerable fervor.[7] If ever in the history of the church there occurred what Henry B. Adams aptly calls a "liturgical subversion of theology," this was it.[8] This gradual but radical change regarding the meaning of the Eucharist is without parallel. Heresies and heretical practices have beset the church from time to time, but sooner or later they were rejected. They were never absorbed and domesticated in the mainstream of Christian thought and cult. However, the beliefs and practices associated with the Eucharist became firmly enshrined in the very structure of the church's cultus and remained unchallenged until the time of the Reformation.

The Reformers purged the cultus of the church of all those elements that were patently contrary to the Scriptures. Even so, the influence of what is commonly called tradition continued to be felt, and it is felt to this day. Protestant Christianity, in line with Luther's appeal to the authority of the Scriptures, has always regarded the Bible as the norm of Christian faith and practice. It must not be assumed, however, that it has been able to bypass tradition. No one can completely ignore history. Every man, every movement is historically conditioned. So is the interpretation of scripture. Persons read and interpret it in the light of their religious and cultural heritage. This must always be taken into consideration.

In the current movement toward an eventual reunion of all branches of Christendom—Eastern Orthodox, Roman Catholic, and Protestant—eucharistic discussions have not figured very prominently thus far. From the Protestant perspective, the papacy and Mariolatry are considered to be the major obstacles to a restoration of the undivided church of the first millenium. However, what may eventually prove to be fully as much a roadblock to reunion as these two issues is the Roman conception of the Eucharist. On this question the testimony of the Scriptures and the theology of the mass are far apart. When the New Testament understanding of the Eucharist is taken seriously, any compromise with the Catholic point of view, or easy accommodation thereto, is out of the question. On this issue Protestant Christianity must take its stand with Luther and declare that unless it can be convinced by the clear testimony of the Scriptures, it will not yield or concede one iota.

viii · THE EUCHARIST: CONTROVERSIAL ISSUES

It is ironic that the most sacred rite of the Christian cultus is also the most divisive factor in Christendom. Perhaps it is divisive for the very reason that it is at the heart of Christian worship. The inability of Christians standing in different traditions to gather as one family around the Lord's table is so well-known that it requires no documentation. This situation has been described as painful and scandalous. Intense and earnest study has been devoted toward clarifying the issues that divide the church in this matter. But in spite of all efforts that have been put forth, the controversial issues are still a long way from being resolved. And they are not likely to be resolved in the near future. Certainly theological inquiry in and by itself is not apt to resolve them.

Nonetheless theological studies, particularly biblical studies, are primary requisites because the church has incorporated in its cultus, beliefs and practices for which there is no principle or precedent in the Scriptures. "The decisive question," says Gustaf Aulén, "is whether that which has been added harmonizes or stands in conflict with the fundamental biblical conception."[1] Even this criterion, excellent as it is, has limitations, for what is found to be in harmony with the Scriptures is affected to a certain extent by a person's point of view, which in turn is conditioned by his theological or ecclesiological heritage.

For instance, it is highly probable that Luther's interpretation of the Lord's Supper was influenced by the Roman doctrine of transubstantiation. Luther, like all men, was a child of his time. Hence, it is by no means improbable that his Catholic heritage influenced his Protestant position. Obviously no one may presume to assert with finality to what extent his doctrine of "in, with, and under," was founded on scripture and to what extent it reflected the revered tradition of the church. That there was an interplay of the two is almost inevitable.

Luther's doctrine of the Lord's Supper is cited here for no other purpose than to illustrate the principle that what is considered to be in harmony with the Word depends on one's starting point. Catholics and Protestants look at the Scriptures through glasses of different tint. Within Protestant Christianity there is a Lutheran point of view and a Reformed point of view; in fact, there are many points of view—conservative and liberal, sacramental and nonsacramental. These chapters also reflect a point of view. This factor must always be taken into account when controversial questions of faith and order are under consideration.

SACRIFICE

One of the eucharistic controversies centers around the question: In what sense is the Eucharist a sacrifice? Is it an atoning sacrifice as it is regarded in Catholic faith, or is it a sacrifice of thanksgiving? The latter view has won widespread support among Protestants. Or should the sacrifice concept be completely dissociated from the Eucharist? This is yet another Protestant point of view.

Sacrifice, in some form or another, has been identified with the Eucharist ever since New Testament times. In the very nature of the case, sacrifice is bound up with the crucial historical moment in which the Lord's Supper has its setting. What Jesus said and did in the Upper Room pointed to his imminent death. His previously uttered declaration that he had come to give "his life as a ransom for many" (Mark 10:45) was now about to be fulfilled. The reference to the cup as "my blood of the covenant, which is poured out for many" (Mark 14:24), is unmistakably sacrificial in essence. Significant, too, is the interpretation that Paul gave to the Lord's Supper. He asks: "The cup of blessing which we bless, is it not a participation in the blood of Christ? The bread which we break, is it not a participation in the body of Christ?" (1 Cor. 10:16). Since Christ offered himself as a sacrifice, the Eucharist which was established just before his death and was intended to memorialize his death might therefore be understood as a participation in his sacrifice. Very much depends, of course, on whether participation is understood in the sense of benefiting from the sacrifice or as enhancing its beneficialness.

In the attempt to arrive at a correct understanding of this particular word of Paul, or for that matter any word about Christ's atoning death, it is important to consider the testimony of the New Testament as a whole. However, the New Testament allows for only one beneficial sacrifice—the one sacrifice that Christ brought when he offered himself. The letter to the Hebrews is explicit and emphatic about this: "When Christ appeared as a high priest of the good things which have come . . . he entered once for all into the Holy Place, taking not the blood of goats and calves but his own blood, thus securing an eternal redemption" (Heb. 9:11-12). This sacrifice need not and cannot be repeated.

Moreover, the redemption that was wrought by the once-for-all sacrifice is God's action, for as Paul succinctly stated, "All this is from God, who through Jesus Christ reconciled us to himself and gave us the ministry of reconciliation; that is, God was in Christ reconciling the world to himself" (2 Cor. 5:18-19). This is a key idea, not only for a correct doctrine of the atonement but also for a proper understanding of the Eucharist. Any belief or presupposition of faith that minimizes God's action in man's redemption is questionable. Equally questionable is any interpretation of the Eucharist that regards it as being in some way "a manifestation in time of the eternal act of Christ as the heavenly High Priest at the altar before the throne of God, perpetually pleading his accomplished and effectual sacrifice." This, according to Aulén, is the position of Dom Gregory Dix.[2] Aulén is fully justified in asking: "Is it biblically legitimate to maintain a continuous offering of Christ in heaven?"[3]

One is also prompted to ask: Is there not something inherently self-contradictory in speaking simultaneously of a "perpetual pleading" and an "accomplished and effectual sacrifice"? If the sacrifice of Christ is accomplished and if it is effectual, must it still be pleaded perpetually? Even more to the point, is it necessary to recall before God his own redemptive action in Jesus Christ? If this is the case, two conclusions seem inevitable: (1) the once-for-all sufficiency of the atonement is abridged; (2) man by implication becomes a contributor to the atonement. The Eucharist recalls for men that God acted decisively in Jesus Christ. This decisive action encompasses the total life and ministry of Jesus along with his death and resurrection. Jesus' death is but one facet of the Christ-event as a whole. If there is any repetitive element to be identified with the Eucharist, it is only in the sense that at each celebration of the sacrament man is confronted anew by God's action in Jesus Christ. In this sense only one may speak of the Eucharist as a re-presentation. And always it should be kept in mind that the sacrifice is God's and not man's.

This basic New Testament principle is easily obscured, particularly by such a phrase as *sacrifice of thanksgiving,* which is common to eucharistic liturgies. Those who celebrate the Lord's Supper have good reason to offer a sacrifice of thanksgiving. Here by visible signs worshipers are confronted in the most dramatic way conceivable by the length, breadth, height, and depth of the love of God. Christ's voluntary sacrifice of himself is the epitome and apex of God's unspeakable love for man. For this reason the celebration of the Eucharist should be an occasion that is not only solemn but also joyous. Unfortunately, very early in the history of the church, the sacrament came to be associated so exclusively with the death of Christ that the resurrection victory, celebrated in apostolic times, was completely overshadowed. Thus it came about that the eucharistic joy of the early church gave way to the eucharistic solemnity that has prevailed in the church ever since.

The Eucharist is indeed an occasion that calls for a sacrifice of thanksgiving. The sacrament itself, however, is not to be considered *our* sacrifice. This is God's sacrifice. It is God's gift to man. He, the Lord, is the host who invites us: "Come, all things are prepared. Taste and see how good the Lord is" (Ps. 34:8). It is noteworthy that in Luther's treatise on the Lord's Supper, written before he became involved in controversies about the sacrament with Zwingli and others, the motif of sacrifice appears to be completely absent. Praise is the dominant motif. The sacrifice motif was introduced later when Luther wrote his two catechisms.

It may be argued that *sacrifice of thanksgiving* as a phrase need not necessarily be encumbered with sacerdotal overtones. Nevertheless, the fact remains that the phrase is ambiguous and may not be as completely free of sacerdotal implications as might be assumed. One petition, commonly found in eucharistic prayers, illustrates the point: "We beseech thee to accept this our sacrifice of praise and thanksgiving, together with the consecration of ourselves unto thee and to thy holy service." The ambiguity centers in the words *this* and *our*. *This* refers to the elements of bread and wine upon which the Holy Spirit has been asked to descend and which is now declared to be *our* sacrifice.

It is meet and proper that we should bring a sacrifice of thanksgiving. "What language shall I borrow to thank thee, dearest Friend?" asked Bernard of Clairvaux in a great hymn attributed to him. Not only what language, but what gift can we offer in gratitude for the divine grace that abounds above our guilt? A verbal sacrifice of thanksgiving is scarcely enough. Only one sacrifice is adequate—the giving of ourselves to him and his service. Nothing less than that will do. Paul was very explicit in this matter. He charged the Christians in Rome to "present your bodies as a living sacrifice, holy and acceptable to God, which is your spiritual worship" (Rom. 12:1).

THE REAL PRESENCE

Inseparably interwoven with the concept of the Eucharist as a sacrifice is the doctrine of the real presence. The Roman Catholic position is well-known. Christ is bodily present in the elements on the altar. The Council of Trent declared "that through consecration of the bread and wine there comes about a conversion of the whole substance of the bread and wine into the substance of the body of Christ our Lord, and of the whole substance of the wine into the substance of his blood."[4] To facilitate the believers' understanding of the miracle of transubstantiation, the church devised the formula which says that, while no substance of the elements remains in the sacrament, the accidents of bread and wine remain; that is, bread and wine continue to look and to taste like bread and wine, but beyond this, they are not what they were before consecration took place.

Protestant teachings concerning the real presence are not as easily set forth. They range all the way from the conservative

Lutheran view of consubstantiation—in, with, and under—to various shades of real, spiritual, and symbolical presence. In general, Protestants are in agreement with the Faith and Order statement of the World Council of Churches: "We all believe that Christ is truly present in the Eucharist, though as to how that presence is manifested and realized we differ."

A belief in the real presence of Christ in or at the Eucharist has prevailed in the church since apostolic times. Whether "the New Testament consistently maintains the real presence of Christ in the Eucharist" in the sense in which this term is normally understood, as Aulén contends, may be an open question. That the pertinent passages in the New Testament readily lend support to this assumption is another matter. In the words of institution—"this is my body"—Luther found the biblical basis for his doctrine of the real presence. The question may well be raised, however, whether in this instance Luther may not have taken the Scriptures too literally, more literally than he generally did. In the heat of a controversy with Zwingli, he appears to have put more weight on the verb *is* than the text warrants.

What must be kept in mind is the fact that the biblical writers commonly used metaphors and similes that can easily be pressed to say more than they were intended to say. The same Lord who said "This is my body" also said, "I am the vine," "I am the good shepherd," "I am the door of the sheep." To take these and other metaphors literally is to do violence to their basic intent. Christ's words of institution have, beyond doubt, become the victims of a totally unwarranted literalism. Aulén's observation at this point is pertinent: "What the Lord says when he gives the bread and wine to his disciples is that he gives himself, his body and blood for them. The interpretive words do not speak about something that is to happen to the bread and wine, but about that which will happen to him."[5]

Two other New Testament passages must also be considered.

In the previous chapter, reference was made to the eucharistic discourse in the Fourth Gospel. The language used there suggests a bodily presence of Christ in the elements: "Unless you eat the flesh of the Son of man and drink his blood, you have no life in you" (John 6:53). But these words cannot be taken literally, for this discourse is a part of the Gospel's general polemic against Docetism. Moreover, as previously noted, the emphasis on eating the flesh and drinking the blood is offset by the declaration that "it is the spirit that gives life, the flesh is of no avail" (John 6:36). Also to be taken into account is the probability that this Gospel may reflect views that stemmed from the cultus of the church toward the close of the first century. By this time the pristine simplicity of the early Christian cultus had been influenced by Hellenism and possibly shaped in part by the priestly strand in Judaism.

The other New Testament source is Paul's account in his first letter to the Corinthians. Two motifs are very much in evidence: one is remembrance and the other is expectation. When the Christians at Corinth observed the Lord's Supper at their weekly love feasts, they were standing midway between the past event of the crucifixion and the coming event of the Lord's return in great power and glory. Expectation was every bit as dominant as remembrance. So confident was the church of the Lord's imminent return that in effect it was already a realized event. Realized eschatology one might call this. He who was coming soon had already come. Under the pressure of persecution, the early Christians foreshortened history even as the apocalyptists of the Old Testament period had done. Thus the historical situation may have been a contributing factor toward the actualization of Christ's presence at the Eucharist.

Aside from what might be called an important footnote to Paul's account of the Eucharist, there is no other scriptural reference that specifically identifies the presence of Christ with the eucharistic elements. In warning against an unworthy participation, the apostle declares that "any one who eats and drinks without discerning the body eats and drinks judgment upon himself" (1 Cor. 11:29). Did Paul mean that Christ's presence was to be discerned in the bread and wine, or did he mean discerning his presence in the body of Christ, namely the church? In view of the friction and the factions that existed within the Corinthian church, the latter must be considered as highly probable. Be that as it may, this one thing is certain: Christ's presence was dynamic, not static; he was present in a living relationship, not in inanimate bread and wine.

Oscar Cullmann and others have pointed out that the Lord's Supper was as much a celebration of Christ's victory over death as it was a commemoration of his death. The certainty of the resurrection, along with the expected Parousia, dominated the cultus of the early church. This is particularly true of the Egyptian liturgy of the Eucharist, which, so scholars tell us, was informed by the resurrection appearances rather than the crucifixion. The *Didache* offers one piece of circumstantial evidence pointing in this direction. A eucharistic prayer, which is here preserved, includes a petition for the Lord's return, "Our Lord, come!" What makes it noteworthy is the fact that this petition was taken over into the Greek language in its original Aramaic form—*Maranatha*. This suggests not only its early origin but also its extensive use in the church.

In view of this, Cullmann's statement—"one ate *with* Christ but did not *eat Christ*"—must be given a high degree of probability. It has the added merit of avoiding the complexities that arise when Christ's presence is identified with the elements. Theoretical questions and metaphysical speculations about the manner and the moment of Christ's presence, which perplexed the church in later centuries, appear to have been unknown in the first century. His presence was real; it was, however, the "realness" of a personal relationship rather than one of literal corporeality.

Over the centuries the theological concern of the church has centered far too much on the manner of Christ's presence in the sacrament. Such concepts as transubstantiation and consubstantiation and various other formulas attempting to spell out the real presence in a substantive way encounter great semantic difficulties. The scholastic distinction between accidents and the substance of the elements is a case in point. It introduces an element of mystification that contributes nothing to the edification of the saints. Protestant attempts to define the real presence in substantive terms fare no better.

The comprehensive survey of Protestant thinking on the nature of Christ's presence in the Eucharist made by Fr. Michael J. Taylor is most enlightening. One notes how language becomes forced and strained when Protestant churchmen attempt to identify the real presence with the elements. Among Lutherans one notes distinctions between a real, a physical, and a sacramental presence, and the lines of demarcation are often difficult to find. Opinions are also divided in regard to the question as to whether the presence of Christ is realized at the moment of consecration or in the moment of reception. While these issues are not nearly as crucial in other Protestant bodies, Fr. Taylor's survey shows very clearly that various shades of opinion prevail within all the denominations he studied. A detailed analysis of the views expressed by those who responded to his questionnaire would take us far beyond the scope of this chapter.[6] It is sufficient to point out, however, that as far as the spiritual vitality of the church is concerned, communion with Christ is more important than a precise understanding of the manner and moment of his presence. To meet the crucified and risen Lord at his table and to be assured of the all-sufficiency of divine grace is more to be desired than to be able to establish or define the how, the when, and the where of his corporeal presence. In the Eucharist we are confronted with a great mystery, but not with magic.

Perhaps the most profitable way of concluding this particular controversial question is to direct attention to the points of agreement reached at Oberlin by the Faith and Order committee that concerned itself with the Eucharist. It is, to be sure, an agreement on minimal terms, but it is a significant agreement nevertheless. The sacrament as set forth in scripture, these churchmen said, has four dimensions: commemoration, participation, proclamation, anticipation.

When Christians come to the Lord's table, they remember that Christ gave his life for man's redemption. It could hardly be otherwise. The very words used in the Upper Room and normally repeated in the eucharistic liturgy point to the crucifixion. In many churches, remembrance is the dominant motif, sometimes the only motif. But whether commemoration is or is not the only motif, the remembered event becomes in effect a present event in the act of being visibly and audibly recalled.

The second dimension is participation. We participate in the sense that we avail ourselves of the divine grace that is freely offered to all who will receive it. When we offer a sacrifice of thanksgiving worthy of the name, we become partners in Christ's redemptive ministry. We who are reconciled now become ambassadors of reconciliation, God making his appeal through us (2 Cor. 5:19-20).

The third dimension is proclamation. According to Paul we "proclaim the Lord's death" as often as we eat the bread and drink the cup (1 Cor. 11:26). This is to say, the observance of the Lord's Supper is a form of Christian witnessing. Christians bear witness to one another, and in so doing strengthen one another in the faith. Indirectly, the eucharistic act is also a witness to those outside the fellowship, for it is a public declaration of faith in and loyalty to the crucified and risen Lord.

The fourth dimension is anticipation. The early church lived on the qui vive of momentarily celebrating the ultimate triumph of the kingdom of God. The Eucharist was but the earthly foretaste of the messianic banquet in the consummated kingdom. This dimension, which was so dominant in the early church, is virtually nonexistent today. We may pray "Thy kingdom come," but we do not really expect it to come. Creedally we may speak of Christ's being present in or at the Eucharist, but unless he is really expected to be present, this affirmation means very little. From the Protestant perspective, a corporeal presence in the elements is a poor substitution for a living, dynamic relationship.

The question might be raised whether the Oberlin conference should not have included a fifth dimension, that of communion. The Eucharist is commonly spoken of as "the bond of (Christ's) living union and fellowship with (his people) to the end of time."[7] Both Luther and Calvin spoke of the sacrament in terms of communion. At this point, whatever their differences may have been on the question of real presence and spiritual presence, they were of one heart and mind. Both regarded the act of eating the bread and drinking the wine to be the outward sign of an inner union with Christ.

This point of view is not without scriptural support. Among the Fourth Gospel's farewell discourses, which have their setting in the Upper Room, we find the parable of the vine and the branches. Union with Christ is its dominant motif. "Abide in me, and I in you" (John 15:4), Jesus is reported to have said. Equally significant is the passage in Revelation 3:20: "Behold, I stand at the door and knock; if any one hears my voice and opens the door, I will come in to him and eat with him, and he with me." Most scholars agree that this word had a sacramental setting. If so, special significance falls on the promise that the living Lord will *eat with* those who invite him to come in. Protestant Christianity is certainly on solid ground when it places the primary emphasis on communion. The advocates of liturgical reform within the Roman Catholic faith are also stressing this aspect of the Eucharist. For this reason they are advocating a freestanding altar, around which, symbolically at least, communicants may gather. The Eucharist then is the means whereby the most intimate communion between Christ and his followers is established.

FREQUENCY

A third controversial issue, less often discussed, centers around frequency of communion. How often is the Eucharist to be observed? In a sense, this is a practical rather than a theological question, yet theology is involved. Considerable uncertainty surrounds this question. This is understandable, for the Scriptures offer no clear and unmistakable guidelines as to when or how often the Lord's Supper is to be observed. Few will dispute that Christians are to "do this in remembrance" of Christ. The dominical origin of this mandate is generally recognized, but this sheds no light on the question of frequency. Nor does the Upper Room setting of the Lord's Supper offer any guidance. If one were to regard the Lord's Supper as the New Testament replacement of the Old Testament Passover, one might even argue in favor of one annual eucharistic observance. However, the dissimilarity between Passover and Eucharist, whatever their original connection, is too great to warrant any such conclusion. If, on the other hand, a kiddush were the occasion on which Jesus and his disciples broke the bread, the conclusion could be drawn that an occasional observance of the Eucharist is in keeping with the dominical intent. The kiddush, not being prescribed by law, was observed when and where a group *(haburah)* was inclined to do so. However, the Lord's mandate "Do this" is far too direct to allow for complete freedom in the matter.

If we turn from the Upper Room setting to the practice of the early church, we gain little by way of an apostolic precedent or principle. In the apostolic period, the Eucharist was the climactic part of the agape. The latter was not a worship service in a contemporary sense. Believers brought their food and also the elements that were used for the Eucharist. When the agape fell into disrepute and was ultimately prohibited, the Eucharist became identified with public worship. It is to be noted, however, that a worship service at that point had two separate parts, each complete in itself—the Liturgy of the Word and the Liturgy of the Upper Room. According to Dom Gregory Dix, it was not until the fourth century that "the two were gradually fused, until they came everywhere to be inseparable parts of a single rite."[8] Tradition, therefore, does not offer a clear directive as to what constitutes authentic Christian practice in this matter.

Even if a standard form of worship had prevailed in the first few centuries, we would still need to take into consideration the fact that the historical situation then was radically different from what it is today. The early church considered itself to be standing midway between the Lord's resurrection and his imminent return. The Eucharist was celebrated in anticipation of his return; in fact, it was looked upon as a foretaste of the messianic banquet in the consummated kingdom. Under the pressure of persecution, the time process was foreshortened to a degree that an anticipated event became a realized event. The church of the twentieth century lives in an entirely different milieu. The ultimate triumph of the coming kingdom is still a valid expectation, but it can hardly be said to be imminent. Certainly it is true that the expectation motif is scarcely more than a marginal note in most eucharistic liturgies of today. One might wish that it were more prominent, but wishing will not make it so. And spelling it out in the liturgy is not apt to change the Christian attitude and outlook.

In support of a service of worship that includes both Word and sacrament, the advocates of liturgical renewal usually invoke the teachings of Luther and Calvin. Neither Reformer, however, was successful in establishing this as the norm. Luther blamed the magistrates and Calvin attributed his failure to the "infirmity and ignorance" of the people. Zwingli, on the other hand, was much less a sacramentalist. He regarded a service of worship to be complete without the sacrament. By and large, Protestant Christianity has followed Zwingli's position. But now the pendulum seems to be swinging toward Luther and Calvin. Liturgical renewal, we are told, calls for a Lord's Day service of Word and sacrament. In Lutheranism, in particular, the objective of the liturgical movement is to restore the Eucharist to the weekly order of worship. The same objective, though less widely supported, can be found in other denominations as well. But if the findings of Fr. Taylor's survey reflect anything like a fair cross section of clerical opinion, the present Protestant practice still commands overwhelming support.

Obviously a question of such great importance is not to be decided by a majority vote. On the other hand, is the majority necessarily in error? Does the weekly observance of the Eucharist belong to the *bene esse* (well being), the *plene esse* (full being), or the very *esse* (being) of a service of worship? It is possible that it belongs to the *bene esse* of worship. Whether it belongs to the *plene esse* of worship is very much an open question, even though the recently published Lord's Day liturgies of the Presbyterian bodies and the United Church of Christ seem to regard it so. In the rubric of both liturgies it is stated: "Properly the Lord's Supper is to be celebrated every Lord's Day." But on what biblical, theological, or traditional grounds can the use of *properly* be justified?

To speak of a worship service without the Eucharist as a "dry mass," as has been done, is first of all to make the mistake of equating worship with the mass and, second, to call into question the validity of Protestant worship as it has been practiced ever since the Reformation. That the mass is the Roman Catholic form of Christian worship is not the issue, nor is the validity of this particular form of worship called into question. But the mass is neither the primitive pattern of Christian worship nor the one and only form of worship.

The point of view maintained here is that liturgical reform tends to become unduly doctrinaire in calling for a weekly Eucharist. Scriptural support for this position is hard to come by. There is no sure word of the Lord to the effect that the sacrament he instituted is to be observed every time his followers assemble on the Lord's Day. No exegetical tour de force will prove that this word of dominical origin—"Do this, as often as you drink it, in remembrance of me" (1 Cor. 11:25)—means every week or that Jesus cannot be remembered in any other way.

Nothing is said about frequency of observance in either Paul's account or in the Gospels. As previously noted, the cultus of the church received only marginal attention in the letters of the New Testament. The emphasis is on the observance of the Eucharist in remembrance of Jesus. And when our Lord's ministry as a whole is taken into account, the emphasis on love and loyalty to him, on doing the will of God, and on the readiness to lose one's life for the sake of the gospel is unmistakable. The force of our Lord's teachings is on the side of the ethical rather than the cultic. This is not to say that the ethical and the cultic are necessarily antithetical. As a matter of fact, many who are working for liturgical reform are doing so because of their evangelical fervor and their social concern. They regard the sacrament to be equally as important to the religious vitality of the church as preaching. The fact that the liturgical movement harbors a goodly number who fuss about liturgical minutiae and all the folderol of clericalism, including vestments, antependia, liturgical colors, genuflections and the like, should not be charged against the movement as such. Liturgical reform should not be judged by its extremes or by its perversions.

Nevertheless, the danger at hand is that sacramentalism easily becomes a substitute for moral earnestness and spiritual depth. Here and there voices are heard echoing the remark of a British churchman, whom Donald Baillie quotes as having said: "To me Christianity is the blessed sacrament."[9] Without in any way questioning the sincerity of those who speak thus, one may nonetheless ask: Is this the essence of Christianity? Does this reflect the mind of Christ? When one recalls the words with which Jesus began his public ministry at Nazareth (Luke 4:18-19) and remembers how he dedicated his time and energy to healing the sick in body, mind, and spirit, one is inclined to say that James came closer to the mind of Christ when he wrote: "Religion that is pure and undefiled before God and the Father is this: to visit orphans and widows in their affliction, and to keep oneself unstained from the world" (Jas. 1:27).

If one judges the Protestant cultus by its fruits—and there is a good dominical precept for applying this criterion (Matt. 7:16)—it can be said in matters of evangelical fervor, social concern, and moral earnestness that religious vitality within Protestant Christianity has not been impaired by what is alleged to be a subordination of the sacrament to the Word. And this can be stated in full recognition of whatever shortcomings Protestant Christianity may have in these areas. To insist therefore, as some do, that a Lord's Day service is incomplete without the Lord's Supper is tantamount to indicting the Protestant cultus since the time of the Reformation.

Similarly, it is difficult to substantiate the claim that the historic pattern of Christian worship calls for both Word and sacrament. It should be stressed that the practice of the primitive church had a different setting and was dominated by a different outlook and an entirely different set of circumstances than those of today. In the post-apostolic period, the Liturgy of the Word and the Liturgy of the Upper Room were not always linked together. Later when the Liturgy of the Upper Room completely absorbed the Liturgy of the Word in the mass, many of the faithful participated as observers, not as communicants. Ever since the Reformation, Protestants have worshiped without including the Lord's Supper in every Lord's Day service, and this too belongs to the historic pattern of Christian worship. As a matter of fact, the actual practice within Protestant Christianity is more definitive of what is historic than any principle laid down by Reformers.

The Joint Committee on Worship of the Presbyterian bodies appears to have taken these factors into account when it declared in its interpretation of the proposed liturgy: "It is by no means the intent of the proposed service to force the celebration of the Lord's Supper every Lord's Day. The frequency of celebration is a question each session must determine in the light of our Lord's command, 'Do this in remembrance of me'" (1 Cor. 11:24). Noteworthy, too, is the statement: "Liturgical renewal is not simply a matter of placing sacred vessels upon a sacred table, or of manipulating and multiplying forms, but rather the effort to bring worship to such a level of reality that it issues in action."

The importance of the Lord's Supper cannot be measured quantitatively. What matters is not how often the sacrament is observed, but rather how reverently, earnestly, and expectantly believers come to the Lord's table. On that score Protestants cannot be found wanting. To observe an average congregation at a communion service is to be convinced that this is indeed a high moment in the church's life of worship. For millions of devout, dedicated churchgoing people, the Lord's Supper is in truth the innermost sanctuary of Christian worship, largely because it is associated with the festive days of the church year—Christmas, Good Friday, Easter, and Pentecost. These are the high points in the church's life. And their significance is heightened when Word and sacrament are conjoined to proclaim the mighty deeds of God in Jesus Christ.

Although the laity of the church may be more or less illiterate in matters of theology and liturgy, Calvin's use of "infirmity and ignorance" to account for the widespread aversion to a weekly eucharistic observance seems rather harsh. It is more likely that lay people are motivated by a fine spiritual sensitivity at this point. They do not want to see reduced to a commonplace something that is high and holy to them. If repentance, reverence, and holy awe were Calvin's primary concern for the celebration of the Lord's Supper, these could easily be lost by instituting a weekly observance. This is by no means a remote or hypothetical possibility. Consider what the regular and repeated use has done to the Lord's Prayer. Used as it is in every Lord's Day service and thoughtlessly recited on many other occasions, its incisive petitions of great concern have become blunted and dulled. Or consider the fate that has befallen the Apostles' Creed. Its regular use has reduced it to an exercise in piety rather than verbalizing the things that are most surely believed.

Some events in life are precious because they are not a part of the daily routine. Holidays, for instance, cast a glow of expectation over the weeks that precede them and an afterglow of radiant recollection over the weeks that follow. The holiness of holidays may lend luster to our everydays. Something similar can be said for the widespread practice of associating the Eucharist with the incarnation, the crucifixion, the resurrection, and the birthday of the Christian church. To these the church might well add Worldwide Communion Sunday to celebrate the growing spirit of ecumenicity, and the anniversary of the Reformation, for this too is a festive day in the Protestant tradition. Or, if it seems more desirable, churches might institute (as some do) a monthly or quarterly observance of the Lord's Supper.

Should the time come when liturgical reform looking toward a "complete" Lord's Day service receives official ecclesiastical endorsement and every congregation is expected to change its form of worship, either in the interest of uniformity or ecumenicity, then a further revision of most liturgies can be expected. A revision of this nature should move first of all in the direction of greater simplicity, such as that which characterizes the eucharistic practice of the Christian Church (Disciples of Christ). Most eucharistic liturgies are unduly ornate, sometimes overlaid with ceremonial pomp and sacerdotal pretensions. It is well to remember that the first Lord's Supper in the Upper Room was observed in austere simplicity. The occasion did not lend itself to liturgical lavishness.

Brevity should also be considered. Altar communion gave way to pew communion largely because of the time required to serve communicants one by one. Anyone who has read or used one of the recently proposed liturgies must have discovered that whatever brevity was gained by pew communion has been lost by the addition of prayers, intercessions, and choral responses. Add to this the rubric suggestion that "a lesson from the Old Testament and a lesson or lessons from the New Testament shall be read,"[10] and the service becomes even longer. James H. Nichols was surely right when he charged the Presbyterian Joint Committee of "pulling our collective leg with its suggestion of *three* readings for a one-hour service."[11]

Theological reorientation is also in order. It is generally agreed that all eucharistic liturgies since Hippolytus are basically centered in the death of Christ with propitiation as the focal point. Such motifs as proclamation, expectation, and fellowship with Christ and with all members of his body, the church, receive only marginal emphasis. Questions can be raised concerning the appropriateness of the kyrie and the Agnus Dei. These carry the sanction of antiquity, but they also reflect a theology that is not altogether biblical. The Scriptures speak very specifically of prevenient grace (Luke 15; Rom. 5:6-11). If prevenient grace means anything, it means that God's forgiveness awaits us before we even ask for it. Is it not then a bit incongruous to plead repetitiously for something that God has in effect already given? All that really remains undone or unfinished is our willingness to receive what is freely offered. Henry B. Adams has correctly observed that a confession of sin is more properly followed by a petition of thanksgiving in acknowledgment of what God has given rather than by a prayer for pardon.[12] Psychologically, there might be some justification for the kyrie or a petition for pardon, for such a verbalization underscores man's readiness to receive what God freely offers; but theologically, a repetitive plea for pardon has the earmarks of liturgical redundancy.

It has also been noted by perceptive churchmen that the Eucharist, which is supposedly a celebration of the whole Christ-event, is so pointedly oriented in the crucifixion that the joy of Christmas and the triumph of Easter are overshadowed by the introspective solemnity of Good Friday. Therefore it may be apropos to suggest that several eucharistic liturgies should be made available, each one specifically adapted for a special festival of the church. Certain elements, such as the words of institution, would be common to all, but beyond this the prayers and intercessions and responses would be specifically appropriate for the festival being observed. The ancient Egyptian liturgy, which was basically informed by Christ's resurrection and his expected return, offers at least a historical precedent for some diversity in eucharistic liturgies.

CONCLUSION

The foregoing suggestions are not intended to embody an exhaustive analysis or critique of existing liturgical forms but merely to indicate that liturgical reform at its present stage of development may not be radical enough to do justice to the biblical understanding of worship, nor realistic enough to speak to twentieth-century man. Reforms initiated thus far have been predominantly eclectic rather than creative. Most revisions borrow heavily from the past instead of attempting to set forth the timeless gospel of God's reconciling act in the idiom of today. It is to be hoped that some day a liturgical commission will be as creative in the matter of liturgical renewal as the Theological Commission of the United Church of Christ was creative in formulating a contemporaneous statement of faith (cf. Appendix). If the temper of the times is as secularized as the death of God theology would have us believe, people of our day are not likely to find meaning in patterns of worship oriented in the classical liturgies of another era. Indeed, it is doubtful whether any liturgical renewal can restore the certainties and convictions which demythologization along with secularization have destroyed.

Just as there is a diversity of gifts within the church, so there should be a diversity of liturgical forms, if for no other reason than to serve people of different temperaments and traditions. There is no biblical precedent or theological justification for any one form of worship. If the Lord of the church could assure the woman of Samaria that the place of worship was unimportant, it may be assumed that he would also regard the manner of worship to be unimportant. Therefore, no attempt should be made to force the church into some kind of liturgical straitjacket. Cultual rigidity has repeatedly eventuated in formalism, ceremonialism, and a loss of religious vitality. It could happen again. "Do not quench the Spirit" (1 Thess. 5:19), Paul admonished the Thessalonians. And he added: "Do not despise prophesying" (1 Thess. 5:20). This means that though a service of worship should be conducted decently and in order, spontaneity and freedom must not be sacrificed. Above all, worship must ever be predicated on sound biblical and theological concepts.

Finally, "until we all attain to the unity of the faith and of the knowledge of the Son of God, to mature manhood, to the measure of the stature of the fullness of Christ" (Eph. 4:13), the church has as much need for both free and fixed forms of worship as it does for both the Word and sacraments. If the purpose of worship is to glorify God, its fruit is man's growth in the grace and the knowledge of the Lord Jesus Christ. Toward that end all worship is directed.

APPENDIX

Statement of Faith

We believe in God, the Eternal Spirit, Father of our Lord Jesus
Christ and our Father, and to his deeds we testify:

He calls the worlds into being,
  creates man in his own image
  and sets before him the ways of life and death.

He seeks in holy love to save all people from aimlessness
  and sin.

He judges men and nations by his righteous will
  declared through prophets and apostles.

In Jesus Christ, the man of Nazareth, our crucified and risen
    Lord,
  he has come to us
  and shared our common lot,
  conquering sin and death
  and reconciling the world to himself.

He bestows upon us his Holy Spirit,
  creating and renewing the church of Jesus Christ,
  binding in covenant faithful people of all ages, tongues,
  and races.

He calls us into his church
  to accept the cost and joy of discipleship,
  to be his servants in the service of men,
  to proclaim the gospel to all the world
  and resist the powers of evil,
  to share in Christ's baptism and eat at his table,
  to join him in his passion and victory.

He promises to all who trust him
  forgiveness of sins and fullness of grace,
  courage in the struggle for justice and peace,
  his presence in trial and rejoicing,
  and eternal life in his kingdom which has no end.

Blessing and honor, glory and power be unto him.   Amen.

NOTES

CHAPTER 1

1. Michael J. Taylor, *The Protestant Liturgical Renewal* (Westminster, Md.: Newman Press, 1963), p. xii.

2. Frederick Herzog, "The Montreal Crisis of Faith and Order," *Theology and Life*, V (Winter, 1963), 315.

3. Pehr Edwall, *Ways of Worship* (New York: Harper & Bros., 1951).

4. *Ecumenical Studies in Worship* (Richmond: John Knox Press, n.d.).

5. *Evangelical and Reformed Catechism* (New Orleans: Rogers Printing Co., 1943), p. 28.

6. *The Service for the Lord's Day* (Philadelphia: Westminster Press, 1964).

7. *The Lord's Day Service* (Philadelphia: United Church Press, 1964).

8. Paul Tillich, "I Decided to Build," *United Church Herald*, VIII (June 15, 1965), 18.

9. T. S. Barrett, *Worship in the Church of South India* (Richmond: John Knox Press, 1958), p. 8.

10. James H. Nichols, "Is the New 'Service' Reformed?" *Theology Today*, XXI (October, 1964), 365.

11. Will Herberg, *Protestant—Catholic—Jew* (Garden City, N.Y.: Doubleday, 1955), p. 96.

12. Gustave Weigel in Taylor, *op. cit.*

13. Henry Bettenson (ed.), *Documents of the Christian Church* (New York: Oxford University Press, 1957), p. 372.

CHAPTER 2

1. Evelyn Underhill, *Worship* (New York: Harper & Bros., 1937), p. 61.

2. Henry Sloane Coffin, *The Public Worship of God* (Philadelphia: Westminster Press, 1946), p. 15.

3. Pehr Edwall, *Ways of Worship* (New York: Harper & Bros., 1951), p. 17.

4. Underhill, *op. cit.*, p. 6.

5. Elmer J. F. Arndt, "Worship and Ethics in Theology," *Theology and Life,* III (November, 1960), 289.

6. Walter Lowrie, *Action in the Liturgy* (New York: Philosophical Library, 1953), p. 119.

7. Wilhelm Hahn, *Worship and Congregation* (Richmond: John Knox Press, 1963), p. 15.

8. Joseph Sittler, "The Shape of the Church's Response in Worship," *The Ecumenical Review,* IX (January, 1958), 141.

9. Underhill, *op. cit.*

10. James Russell Lowell, "The Vision of Sir Launfal," part 2, stanza 8.

11. Coffin, *op. cit.*

12. Underhill, *op. cit.*, p. 5.

13. Coffin, *op. cit.*, p. 24.

14. Edwall, *op. cit.*, p. 32.

15. Hahn, *op. cit.*, p. 28.

16. Willard Learoyd Sperry, *Reality in Worship* (New York: Macmillan, 1947), p. 258.

17. John A. T. Robinson, *Honest to God* (Philadelphia: Westminster Press, 1963).

CHAPTER 3

1. Alfred Lord Tennyson, "The Higher Pantheism," stanza 6.

2. Millar Burrows, *An Outline of Biblical Theology* (Philadelphia: Westminster Press, 1946), p. 68.

3. J. Coert Rylaarsdam, "The Matrix of Worship in the Old Testa-

ment," *Worship in Scripture and Tradition,* ed. Massey H. Shepherd, Jr. (New York: Oxford University Press, 1963), p. 53.

4. *Ibid.,* p. 62.

5. John Wick Bowman, *Prophetic Realism and the Gospel* (Philadelphia: Westminster Press, 1955), p. 164.

CHAPTER 4

1. Friedrich Heiler, *The Spirit of Worship* (London: Hodder & Stoughton, Ltd., 1926), p. 21.

2. Dom Gregory Dix, *The Shape of the Liturgy* (Naperville, Ill.: Alec R. Allenson, Inc., 1960), p. 36.

3. Franklin W. Young, "The Theological Context of New Testament Worship," *Worship in Scripture and Tradition,* ed. Massey H. Shepherd, Jr. (New York: Oxford University Press, 1963), p. 78.

4. Scott Brenner, *The Way of Worship* (New York: Macmillan, 1960), p. 106.

5. *Ibid.,* p. 118. Italics added.

6. Walter Lowrie, *Action in the Liturgy* (New York: Philosophical Library, 1953), p. 159.

7. Evelyn Underhill, *Worship* (New York: Harper & Bros., 1937), p. 39.

8. *Ibid.,* p. 27, quoting S. Boulgakoff, *L'Orthodoxie,* p. 196.

9. Cyril C. Richardson, "Some Reflections on Liturgical Art," *Union Seminary Quarterly Review,* IX (March, 1953).

10. Paul Tillich, *The Protestant Era* (Chicago: University of Chicago Press, 1948), pp. 94, 112.

11. Paul Tillich, *The Interpretation of History* (New York: Charles Scribner's Sons, 1936), pp. 52 f.

CHAPTER 5

1. Henry Sloane Coffin, *The Public Worship of God* (Philadelphia: Westminster Press, 1946), pp. 82 f.

2. Morgan Phelps Noyes, *Prayers for Services* (New York: Charles Scribner's Sons, 1934), p. 137.

3. E. J. F. Arndt, "Worship and Ethics in Theology," *Theology and Life,* III (November, 1960), 289.

4. Alexander Schmemann, "Theology and Liturgical Tradition," *Worship in Scripture and Tradition,* ed. Massey H. Shepherd, Jr. (New York: Oxford University Press, 1963), p. 173.

5. Martin Luther, "Appeal to the German Nobility," *Luther's Works,* ed. Jaroslav Pelikan, trans. Martin H. Bertram (St. Louis: Concordia Publishing House, 1958).

CHAPTER 6

1. Horton Davies, *Christian Worship—Its History and Meaning* (Nashville: Abingdon Press, 1957), p. 31.
2. Donald Baillie, *The Theology of the Sacraments* (New York: Charles Scribner's Sons, 1957), p. 96.
3. "What Mary Means to Protestants," *Time* (September 11, 1964), 58.
4. John Calvin, *Institutes of the Christian Religion,* ed. John T. McNeil (Philadelphia: Westminster Press, 1960).
5. *Book of Worship* (St. Louis: Eden Publishing House, 1947), p. 96.
6. *Book of Worship for Free Churches* (New York: Oxford University Press, 1948), p. 327.
7. Joseph Sittler, *The Ecology of Faith* (Philadelphia: Muhlenberg Press, 1961), p. 100.
8. Frederick Herzog, "The Norm and Freedom of Christian Worship," *Worship in Scriptures and Tradition,* ed. Massey H. Shepherd, Jr. (New York: Oxford University Press, 1963), p. 125.

CHAPTER 7

1. *Evangelical and Reformed Catechism* (New Orleans: Rogers Printing Co., 1943), p. 28.
2. In early printings, *The Revised Standard Version of the Bible* reads at 1 Corinthians 11:24: "This is my body which is broken for you." A footnote to that passage indicates that many authorities omit *broken* and that a few read *given.* Later printings omit *broken* from this passage which now reads: "This is my body which is for you." A note at this point explains that other ancient authorities read *broken for.*
3. Oscar Cullmann and F. J. Leenhardt, *Essays on the Lord's Supper,* trans. J. G. Davies (Richmond: John Knox Press, 1958), p. 12.
4. *Ibid.,* p. 13.
5. Henry Bettenson (ed.), *Documents of the Christian Church* (New York: Oxford University Press, 1947), p. 372.
6. Thomas J. O'Brien, *An Advanced Catechism* (Chicago: John B. Oinx, n.d.), p. 12.

7. B. S. Easton (ed.), *Apostolic Tradition of Hippolytus* (Hamden, Conn.: Shoe String Press, n.d.).

8. Henry B. Adams, "Liturgical Subversion of Theology," *The Pulpit,* XXXV (June, 1964), 7.

CHAPTER 8

1. Gustaf Aulén, *Eucharist and Sacrifice* (Philadelphia: Muhlenberg Press, 1958), p. 61.

2. Dom Gregory Dix, *The Shape of the Liturgy* (Naperville, Ill.: Alec R. Allenson, Inc., 1960), p. 49.

3. Aulén, *op. cit.*

4. Henry Bettenson (ed.), *Documents of the Christian Church* (New York: Oxford University Press, 1947), p. 370.

5. Aulén, *op. cit.*, p. 158.

6. Michael J. Taylor, *The Protestant Liturgical Renewal* (Westminster, Md.: Newman Press, 1963).

7. *Book of Worship for Free Churches* (New York: Oxford University Press, 1948).

8. Dix, *op. cit.*, p. 37.

9. Donald Baillie, *The Theology of the Sacraments* (New York: Charles Scribner's Sons, 1957), p. 92.

10. *The Lord's Day Service* (Philadelphia: United Church Press, 1964), p. 10.

11. James H. Nichols, "Is the New 'Service' Reformed?" *Theology Today,* XXI (October, 1964), 365.

12. Henry B. Adams, "Liturgical Subversion of Theology," *The Pulpit,* XXXV (June, 1964), 7.